THE HIDDEN
MESSAGES IN
FOOD

*Use Your Relationship with Food to
Unlock Your True Potential*

TERI MOSEY

BALBOA
PRESS

A DIVISION OF HAY HOUSE

Balboa Press books may be ordered through booksellers or by contacting:

Balboa Press
A Division of Hay House
1663 Liberty Drive
Bloomington, IN 47403
www.balboapress.com
1 (877) 407-4847

Print information available on the last page.

ISBN: 978-1-9822-0112-8 (sc)
ISBN: 978-1-9822-0114-2 (hc)
ISBN: 978-1-9822-0113-5 (e)

Library of Congress Control Number: 2018903844

Balboa Press rev. date: 03/29/2018

For my New York family and friends

CONTENTS

INTRODUCTION

My Story

Sometimes life gets turned upside down and you are forced to reexamine the direction you've been going in. That happened for me the day I was admitted to the emergency room of my local hospital, knowing that something—but not *what*—was seriously wrong with me.

At thirty, with an outer appearance of being healthy and fit, I struggled to catch my breath, as longtime anxiety attacks continually plagued me. In addition, I was chronically exhausted and now dealing with a frightening new symptom, heart palpitations.

If you've ever had to stay in a hospital for any period of time, you know it's a scary and humbling experience. After being admitted to the ER, I was put on the cardiovascular floor and monitored for a potential heart attack. I was terrified.

Although I had spent years helping others on their path to wellness as a health and nutrition educator, it was only when I got sick myself with no clear diagnosis that I started on a personal journey to heal myself.

That journey healed me and transformed my life.

Turns out that the frightening hospital experience was exactly what I needed to begin making a major shift in how I was living. I guess there is validity in the saying that illness is Western society's form of meditation, forcing us to search within and come to terms with our life choices. For me, that inward search took the form of exploring my relationship with food and health and applying what I learned to the daily choices I made. Ultimately, that search led me to place where I got to know my authentic self.

A Leap into the Unknown

In hindsight, I was given many signals that I needed to reset my life's course. Like so many people, I was partly content with where I was and partly afraid of taking a leap into the unknown. I knew new choices would change everything about my life, from my relationships to the direction of my career to where I wanted to live. It would be a big leap for me, but in retrospect, it was one very much worth taking.

The biggest step was shifting my perspective. Because I'd majored in biochemistry and physiology in college, my initial exposure to the world of nutrition was filled with memorizing the parts of the digestive system, comprehending the essential nutrients of protein and carbohydrates, and learning a never-ending list of vitamins and minerals. My studies were concentrated on the human body structure, from anatomy to chemical composition, as I learned the pathways and physiological functions necessary to get my degree. Everything I studied was neatly organized in systems with strictly defined boundaries, making it manageable and easy to navigate. I was building a strong base of knowledge on how the body functions from the view of physical matter, and I embraced modern science's established method of scientific inquiry that relied solely on physical observations. Credibility and validation are the gold standard in the mainstream approach, and anything that does not fit this criteria is dismissed and in some circles mocked as quackery or nonsense.

This materialistic view became my own personal belief system for many years, limiting me to see the body as a machine. I was disciplined and linear in my thinking, a perspective that kept anything like emotion and spirituality out of the operations of everyday life. As I look back, I recognize how inflexible, like the scientific view, my nature was. I saw nutrition and the health industry—*life*, for that matter—in black-and-white terms, and I was quick to categorize and label it all with calculated responses that left little room for change or creativity.

Boy, did I follow the rules! I personally strived for concrete evidence, dismissing what did not fit the modern science criteria. For years I operated within this perspective, and it worked—sort of. As a wellness consultant, I guided my clients in nutrition and exercise at the level of understanding I had. I could deliver a successful presentation to health organizations with passion and enthusiasm, giving 100 percent of what I had in that moment. My life from the outside looked pretty good—yet it wasn't.

Lying there in the hospital bed on the cardiovascular ward, being subjected to test after test for my heart, I finally reached the point where I was ready to accept and even welcome change into my life. Fortunately, I didn't suffer a heart attack and was released from the hospital with a stern warning to reduce stress in my life. But my journey of transformation that began that day took me beyond simply reducing my stress. The deeper change came as I shifted my perspective and stopped analyzing and compartmentalizing everything. It started when I got out of my head and *into my body*, a new place for me, where getting healthy meant I had to *feel* more and *think* less.

My Transformative Journey

Looking back, I can see that the journey of my transformation clearly unfolded in three distinct stages, each one building on and leading naturally to the next. Starting out, it was a shift in my perspective on food that initially made the greatest difference. For years my food choices had been purely intellectual. In keeping with my training, I dissected food into its individual components, estimated caloric content, and even plugged numbers into equations to estimate metabolic rate. I stayed with this mainstream approach for myself, my clients, and my students because it was logical and gave me a sense of control.

But the healing process I began after my crisis introduced me to another world. In my search for solutions to my many troublesome symptoms, I became exposed to the energetic component of food and the human body. This was something my training had not covered at all but now was taking me beyond measuring food in terms of calorie and scale to meet food in its fuller potential.

I continued to expand my knowledge and experience as I sought out various healing modalities that had been foreign to me before, including Traditional Chinese Medicine. I learned how I am connected to my external environment and to the seasons, advancing my perspective to a second stage of experiencing my authentic self as part of something greater than my small ego. I began to see possibilities in life that I would never have imagined had I stayed in my narrow world.

My perspective and relationship with food continued to expand as I traveled through the first two stages, not realizing they were preparing me for what was to come in a third stage in which I was exposed to spirituality. I studied Ayurveda, meditation, yoga, energy medicine, and even medical intuition, past-life regression, and spirituality. I was introduced to the chakras, a subject that instantly resonated with me.

At first I met these ideas and approaches with skepticism, even downright doubt. I thought, *You're going to poke me with needles and move my what? What do you mean I have "excessive wind"? Chakras? I don't see any energy centers in my body!* But gradually I started to thrive on these new ideas through reading, one-on-one sessions with practitioners, retreats and workshops, and completing extensive training programs. I started having acupuncture sessions, followed by taking yoga on the beaches of the south shore of Long Island and attending presentations given by medical intuitive Caroline Myss on energy work with the chakras.

My health improved, and my experience of life became lighter, less anxious, and more fun. Not surprisingly, what I was discovering had more to do with my personal growth than simply my physical symptoms. I began to see many aspects of myself I was not aware of or had silenced in an attempt to avoid. I went from a life being ruled by insecurities and codependence to one ruled by an unwavering inner courage and resilience. Along with understanding myself, I came to understand others better. I stopped blaming others and playing the role of the victim. Now I increasingly looked within to find my answers and solutions.

My personal growth took a quantum leap as I moved through the third stage of my journey and began to embrace the world of spirituality. My study of the chakras, those energy centers in the body that link us with universal consciousness, gave me a way to connect the dots in my life and make sense of what I was experiencing. There were many aha moments, times when I was confronted with unexpressed emotions and needs, leading to a heightened level of awareness. It was a humbling experience, in which I endured moments of isolation and loneliness before an all-encompassing feeling of connection and oneness became my new normal.

My Life Today

It took me almost forty years of living to arrive at a place where I could make the choice to live authentically. Still a work in progress, I now experience clarity of mind, an unimagined inner grounding, and a deep connection to my peaceful warrior within. I see the world as my playground and don't hesitate to say, "Bring it on, Universe!" How I found myself was through a multitude of experiences that went from relying on my scientifically driven mindset to accepting of my energetic being to finally embracing the wisdom of the hidden messages in food.

Today I remain fascinated by understanding the intricate workings of the human body, all the way down to the chemicals and receptors on each of our fifty trillion cells. I continue to grow and learn because of the incredible advancements in research and technology that are reported daily. The difference is I now look for connections and relationships where I once saw separation and fixed boundaries. Seeing life as connected, not divided into separate pieces, actually helps me release my anxiety, a state of mind I'd previously accepted as normal, even though at times it was debilitating.

When something is that life changing, it needs to be shared. *The Hidden Messages in Food* presents a transformative approach to diet and nutrition, one that can shift your fundamental relationship with food and life as you move through the three stages I experienced and lay out for you in this book. Within these pages is an opportunity for you to develop a healthy relationship with food and heal challenges you may have—anxiety and depression, hormone imbalances, chronic digestive issues, weight struggles, and low immunity, to name but a few—that have plagued you for years.

Please accept my invitation to take this journey and regain your natural health. And along the way, don't be surprised if you gradually evolve into who you really are—your authentic self.

What Food Has Taught Me

My evolving relationship with food has changed my life profoundly. Now, living the journey, I have

- healed my chronic health issues, including heart troubles and anxiety;
- learned to feel more connected to others;
- expanded my ability to be in relationships;
- become more playful and expressive;
- become more grounded while at the same time feeling freer;
- found inner peace;
- gained confidence in myself and my purpose;
- discovered a willingness to step outside my comfort zones;
- rekindled my creativity; and
- learned to live life through the eyes of gratitude.

PROLOGUE TO THE JOURNEY

Calories, protein, low fat, no fat—the sheer number of diet approaches being promoted on the market today is enough to make your head spin. Whether it is weight loss, a health issue, or just keeping yourself fit and healthy, there's a food plan for every need. Each promise to deliver a quick fix, as if you were a machine in dire need of repair—not a human being.

But you are not a machine, as our Western paradigm of health and medicine has led us all to believe, and we don't need yet another dietary prescription based on the outdated mechanical model. Instead, it is time for an entirely new way to relate to food that fits a more updated, twenty-first-century, mind-body model of our human physiology.

In this book, you will learn a new way to make food choices that personally fit your true nature—who you are as a *whole* human being, body, mind, and soul. The pathway I am introducing you to will resolve health issues you have—and, along the way, transform your life on many levels.

A New Relationship with Food

Transforming your relationship with food has a lot to do with perspective. When you shift how you see food, you shift how you relate to it, and as a result you are empowered to make healthier food choices. Your priorities, passions, and aspirations are automatically rearranged. Your entire life starts to change, and at a most fundamental level, a new you emerges.

On your journey to shift your relationship with food, you will travel, as I did myself, through three distinct stages, each one marking an increase in awareness of your ever-evolving needs. At each stage, you will have a chance to ask yourself questions for self-assessment and reflection in order to assist in the process.

Shifting your relationship with food is a way of taking a closer look at how you live on all levels. The food you eat is so much more than fuel for your body and calming for your grumbling stomach. In a new relationship, weight loss is not about counting calories or being obsessed with numbers on a scale, nor is there a universal program for addressing these challenges that is suitable to all. The concept of health is so much bigger than the next weigh-in, this month's superfood, or the latest flab-reducing exercise system. While food's true significance may be hidden in the shadows of today's towering, quick-fix health and diet market, the messages food has for you are so much deeper and worthier of your attention and appreciation.

Food nourishes *all* of you—body, mind, and soul. This holistic perspective I am advocating will challenge the beliefs, attitudes, and actions you may have toward food and, on a grander scale, toward your life. You will leave your old views behind and enter a period that is unknown and unpredictable. Embarking on such a journey puts you in a place of vulnerability and asks you to address all aspects of who you are, not just your immediate thoughts of what to buy for dinner and planning meals.

You may have heard the saying "Life begins at the end of your comfort zone." And that certainly applies to what I am inviting you to explore in this book. But all that is required is keeping your mind open to a different perspective. This is just the beginning of the realization that you are in the driver's seat, cocreating your health and ultimately your life.

A Holistic Perspective: What It Means

Holistic is such a trendy word these days. When I ask people what their perception of holistic is, the responses often include "living naturally," "being healthy," "organic," and "eating clean." It's clear that the media and marketing has brought the term, but not necessarily the depth of the concept, into mainstream language.

In its deeper meaning, holistic refers to connection and wholeness. It implies interconnectedness and interrelationships continuously occurring within the human body and between all living beings. In terms of the human body, holistic means that all aspects of who you are—body, mind, and soul—are connected and continuously influencing one another.

Fundamental to a holistic perspective is the merging of Eastern and Western worldviews. In the West, our modern science concentrates on physical matter, fitting predictable laws within a reductionist method of inquiry. Eastern teachings point in a different direction. They invite the intangibles into the story, including seeing humans as beings of energy, and bring the inner emotional and spiritual worlds into the picture. Holistic represents a blend of all that we are, making it a complete and empowering perspective.

Holistic doesn't mean you focus solely on Eastern teachings and disregard all the scientific discoveries and technological advances that our modern Western science has achieved. It also doesn't mean to undermine, dismiss, or in some cases mock thousands of years of ancient wisdom because that wisdom doesn't fit into the modern world's idea of scientific inquiry and validity. Both systems have merit and together represent the whole of nature and the workings of the human body as well as food/nutrition's characteristics and domain.

Entering the holistic perspective, blending the physical with the energetic, you begin to see that your mind and body are not separate but one interrelated system or network. Medical researchers are finding connections between the body and mind that demonstrate a network of information with no fixed edges. Each system, organ, and gland, down to the tiny individual cells, are all in communication with one another. We may be able to look at an organ after dissection and see its physical boundaries, but when it is in an animated physical body, that organ communicates with all other parts, and every entity is connected and affected by the others.

Such a unified paradigm of life can be referred to as *mind-body wholeness*. This is an essential understanding to have if you are going to shift your relationship with food and start seeing the true potential that nutrition and diet can have in your life.

Mind-Body Pioneers

Dr. Candace Pert was one of the first neuroscientists to recognize that the brain and immune system communicate on a molecular level. Pert and her immunologist husband, Michael Ruff, studied the chemical links between physical cell structures and emotional experiences. By initially studying the receptors on the surface of cells, they found neuropeptide receptors throughout the body, not just in the brain. Emotions, which in scientific terms are the vibratory link of an informational substance and cell receptor, exist in the body at the cellular level. Every molecule of emotion found in the limbic center of the brain, where you store your past experiences and emotions, is also found in the body, including the gut. Emotions and experiences are intertwined, which is why you can at times recall a past experience and literally feel like you are reliving it.

In her book *Molecules of Emotion*, Pert spoke of informational substances known as neuropeptides, their impact on physiology, and how they are the biochemical link between the mind and body, forming a communication system she referred to as the psychosomatic network. Her groundbreaking work initiated a new branch of science called psychoneuroimmunology, or PNI, linking scientific disciplines that were traditionally viewed separately. Her work validated what has been known for thousands of years—that our bodies are not just hunks of flesh and bones, but intelligent systems capable of healing and transforming.

Author and cell biologist Bruce Lipton, known for his work in epigenetics, also writes and lectures on the mind-body connection. Epigenetics is the science of how our environment influences the expression of our genes. Going back to the 1800s, when DNA was first identified as a distinct molecule, it's been the belief of most scientists that our genes control our biology and that any individual responsibility for our health is out of our hands. It wasn't until after discoveries made by the Human Genome Project in the 1990s that scientists concluded our complexity did not come from our genes alone, since we have only one thousand more genes than a worm! Other factors must be at work.

It soon became understood what those factors are. Genes are not self-activating, meaning they cannot turn themselves on and off. Instead, proteins that are triggered by environmental signals determine which genes will be expressed to determine health or disease. These environmental signals can be in the form of our thoughts, emotions, nutrition, lifestyle choices, and stress management.

Through Lipton's research, described in his book *The Biology of Belief,* he found that each of the fifty trillion cells in our bodies is an intelligent entity that contains all the systems the body has as a whole. All cells are capable of respiration, digestion, excretion, and communication with the external environment through receptors on the cell membrane. Through his continuing research, he demonstrates that our minds or beliefs are powerful determiners of our health and well-being.

Finally, I want to mention the work of world-renowned medical intuitive / spiritual director Caroline Myss, who worked with Dr. Norm Shealy, a neurosurgeon and pioneer in pain management. They reported that we carry in our energetic beings and store in our bodies' tissues all of who we are—that our biology reflects our biographies. To read their combined work in *Creation of Health* and her *Anatomy of Spirit* is an eye-opening excursion into the connections between our energetic and physical beings. Myss went so far as to add an element of spirituality, linking our energy centers described in Eastern medicine as chakras to provide another piece of the grand picture of the holistic human experience.

Candace Pert, Bruce Lipton, and Caroline Myss—each one of these individuals traveled their own personal journeys to discover and validate that mind and body are indeed one, not separate entities existing apart from each other. As each chose his or her path, bravely willing to oppose mainstream trends, they opened up opportunities for a more expansive life to all of us.

Today, you and I no longer live in the rigid material world of the eighteenth-century scientist Isaac Newton. Some laws from his time still hold (gravity, for example!), but the current worldview has shifted significantly from his time. We now live in a post-Einstein world governed more by the laws of quantum physics than Newtonian laws. In the quantum world, the beliefs and expectations of a person observing any event or phenomenon actually influence what the outcome will be. We now have proof that there is an energetic and biomolecular side to living beings, and both views are complementary.

Overview of the Journey

Within these pages is a way of living for those who seek guidance but not rules. A fundamental concept underlying this journey is that there is no one in the world exactly like you, and so conformity to prescribed dietary regimens can never work. You are completely unique, and this is true on every level of your being. Your entire makeup, including biochemical, physiological, emotional, and intellectual constitution, along with your life's purpose, is completely unique to you. Whatever you need, wish, or seek are all aspects of your unique being. One size does *not* fit all.

In the journey you are about to begin, you will find information and exercises that will provoke internal questions that only you can answer. From your own answers, the realization of your true potential and the limitless possibilities available to you will arise.

The journey, exploration, and transition are where you will recognize what you need, what works for you and meets your uniqueness. Without actually going through a transformative process, true change cannot occur. The journey is what healing and evolving is all about. Eating and your relationship with food can be your pathway there.

The holistic approach asks you to step away from old beliefs based on mainstream trends with their sole focus on the physical body and lessen the literal analytical thinking of the left brain. It asks you to stop labeling people, food, or health approaches as good or bad, giving everything a fixed or permanent meaning.

Are you up for that? I hope so, because it can turn your life upside down and inside out—as it did mine. This journey through nutrition is actually your life's journey to discover your authentic self. It's not a thirty-day or eight-week diet program for you to accomplish so that a few months or years later, you can go back to what got you in trouble in the first place. It's the recognition of the need for true change. It's a willingness to create a new reality—from the inside out.

The transformational journey ahead will ask you to engage in conscious living. This means a willingness to actively participate in your own healing process. The concept of healing is an internal process that asks for exploration of all your conditioned beliefs, attitudes, and behaviors. Through an expanded state of awareness, you can begin to understand that all your thoughts, words, and actions impact your internal health, as well as your experience in the physical world. And the cherry on top of living authentically is that when you do, you give others the courage to do the same.

What's Next …

Understanding the hidden messages in food and shifting your relationship with food happens in three distinct stages, each one adding an additional layer of understanding and experience in your journey. In stage 1, you explore the full potential of food physically and energetically, expanding your perspective to include your unique state of mind and body in the health equation. Then in stage 2, you add another layer of understanding, learning to use nature as your guide to find your true connection with the external world. You are a miniature version of the universe, and everything happening outside of you is a reflection of your own inner workings. Through the observation of nature and the change in seasons, you can begin to understand the ancient art of living that allows you to live in harmony with the world.

Stage 3 focuses on the deepest layer of food's hidden messages, connecting the food to the seven energy centers in your body, known in the Eastern view as chakras. You will examine your intentions, cravings, and relationship to eating that can be traced back to a universal source and provide meaning for your life. Food recommendations, self-reflection questions, and complementary physical and lifestyle exercises will support you as you begin climbing the ladder of the chakras from bottom to top, and, in the process, transform your relationship with food. As you move along on your journey, you will be empowered to see the food you eat become an evolutionary instrument for discovering and evolving your authentic self.

STAGE 1

FOOD BEYOND THE CALORIE

In stage 1 of your transformational journey through food, you expand your perspective on food beyond the narrow physical measurements of calorie and scale to encompass a more holistic perspective. This new view of food shows you food's full potential to aid you in accomplishing your health and well-being goals.

Creating this fuller understanding of food will do two things for you. First, you will be better equipped at deciphering the difference between what advertising tells you and the real nutritional value of food. A simple fact is we all need to eat, making us all consumers. None of us are immune to the persuasion of the newest health trends, magic foods, or quick-fix diet plans that prey on our limited knowledge. Second, with a fuller understanding, you can put the more conventional knowledge into a new context, one that includes the personal variable and essential element—*you*!

It doesn't matter what you eat if you don't include *who* is eating—body, mind, and soul. Your whole self matters. It's time to look beyond the limits of the physical body and into the bigger picture of how who you are is related to everything else, not isolated and divided into parts like a machine. Without embracing your wholeness, goals of health, longevity, and weight loss will continue to be achieved short term but remain largely unattainable.

Through the stages of this journey, you will come to see that food and your relationship to eating reflects who you are and how you live. From a salt craving or aversion to bitter flavors to closet eating or whether you take the time to make an elaborate home-cooked meal just for yourself, this says volumes on a deeper level. There lie the hidden messages in food, seeing past the food's characteristics to view how and what you eat in relationship to yourself and the world.

All healthy relationships require the ability to be flexible and respond to change. Your personal nutrition needs evolve and change through your natural life cycle and as life circumstances arise. What you needed when you were ten, twenty-five, or sixty-five is not the same. If you are beginning to incorporate exercise into your life or compete in your first marathon, have developed heart disease, or perhaps are dealing with the challenge of cancer, your dietary pattern will alter in accordance with your circumstances. The journey of transforming your relationship with food asks you to incorporate more flexibility and right-brain thinking in your life.

In stage 1, we expand our knowledge of food first through an understanding of the physical properties of food, then the energetic characteristics, and finally the environment in which we eat our meals.

CHAPTER 1

THE PHYSICAL POTENTIAL OF FOOD

The most basic trait of any food is its physical qualities. Here we find four essential properties: caloric content, chemical composition, acid/alkaline balance, and impact on gene expression. All of these need to be considered in the context of mind-body wholeness in order for you to make any decision about a food's impact on your diet and nutrition. The current approach of the Western paradigm has been to concentrate on a single element, leading to confusion and misleading myths. Emphasis on the calorie as the be-all and end-all for choosing food on a weight-loss diet is a perfect example.

The Infamous Calorie

The focus of modern nutrition's approaches to health and weight management is on the infamous calorie. The calorie has taken the spotlight and is continuously overemphasized, leading to many people struggling with their relationship with food. Perhaps you can personally relate. So many clients—too many to count—have used the calorie as the sole means for choosing foods, regardless of the ingredients, quality, or processing. As long as they could count the calories, that was all that mattered. Unfortunately, with their lifelong weight struggles and growing list of health ailments, this approach is not working.

What exactly is a calorie? It is a unit of energy. You need calories (energy) in order to live. The foods you eat provide the energy for every system in your body to operate, both biologically and psychologically.

The theory behind counting calories as a way to define and make food choices is incredibly misleading, especially when all other food characteristics are dismissed. Going back to the 1800s, a chemist named Wilbur Olin Atwater studied the dynamics of energy metabolism and created a system to calculate the number of calories in carbohydrates, proteins, and fats. This data was then translated to what is now our present-day marketing strategy for food education and sales. For example, you may have heard of carbohydrates and proteins yielding four calories per gram while fats yield nine calories per gram. It sounds straightforward. Just count calories and then work the numbers: calories consumed to calories expended. *If I manage the calorie equation, I'll be healthy and maintain my desired body weight.*

If only it were that simple.

Let's peel away the layers of this calorie myth and see what we find. First, not all energy that is consumed is digested and absorbed. Calculating food in a laboratory by measuring the heat released as the food burns does not produce the same outcome as when the food is being processed through the digestive tract. Many factors determine how much energy will be used to process the food versus how much may be available for absorption. This means the calories listed on food packaging labels are only guesstimates with a large range of inaccuracy.

In addition, no two foods, alike or different, with the same estimated caloric content are actually the same once inside the body. One hundred calories of cooked carrots to one hundred calories of raw carrots is different. One hundred calories of chocolate chip cookies and one hundred calories of broccoli are also not the same. Food is so much more than its caloric content!

Furthermore, each food has its own dietary or chemical signature to it. This means that inside your body, food has a specific vibrational frequency and essence. Look at protein. Theoretically, protein is calculated to provide you with four calories per gram. But eating protein in the form of cow's milk and eating plant protein from lentils is not the same. Not only does each food have different digestive and metabolic effects on the body, but they contain hundreds of other nutrients and compounds that play a part in the digestion and assimilation of the food.

Now let's make this more personal. Remember it's not just what food you are eating; it's also who is eating the particular food and all the variables that individual brings to the equation. Eating is not a laboratory experiment, and we can't detach the process of digestion from the actual person who is consuming the food. As a human being, you may have similar body structures, organs, and systems to others, but how your body operates in order to carry out its functions is distinctive to *you*.

This concept of personal variables was understood for thousands of years in ancient teachings and was coined *biochemical individuality* by Dr. Roger Williams in 1956. Williams stated,

> While the same physical mechanisms and the same metabolic processes are operating in all human bodies, the structures are sufficiently diverse that the sum total of all reactions taking place in one individual's body may be very different from those taking place in the body of another individual of the same age, sex and body size.

This biochemical diversity Williams was pointing to is reflected in the body's ability to detoxify, control blood cholesterol, metabolize nutrients, regulate blood sugar levels, and manage long-term weight.

Everyone has a unique biochemical makeup and a unique emotional constitution, genetic inheritance, and lifestyle factors that influence their overall health and well-being. Simply, everyone's digestive system operates differently. From chewing, stomach acidity, release of digestive enzymes, and friendly gut bacteria to the individual's state of mind, levels of stress, and immunity status—all of these factors influence the digestion and absorption of foods.

You can see how the impact on your body of a particular food goes far beyond a singular calorie measurement!

We've all been in that space where we have attempted to count every calorie that we consumed. Unfortunately, in working with my clients, I have witnessed how counting every calorie consumed can actually prevent a healthy, genuine relationship with food, leading to a complete disregard for any other aspect or possible nourishment a food can provide.

Many clients would count calories and midday hop on the scale, looking for it to tip in their favor. I'm sure you can imagine the daily frustration and hysteria as the scale toyed with their emotions. There was also the act of saving calories for a big event and a willingness to limit meals to low-cal but highly processed food choices, trading quality for possible weight loss. This often resulted in a decline in overall vitality, a lack of weight management, onset of chronic illness, and depressed states of mind.

There are too many people living in this roller-coaster diet world. Through the holistic paradigm, the merging of ancient wisdom, and current scientific observations, we now know better. Food and eating are meant to be part of a way of living, a free-flowing, evolving art. I wonder, with the continued scientific knowledge of the misrepresentation and inaccuracy of caloric counting, whether an upheaval of the nutrition standards on a grander scale will manifest in our lifetime.

Carbohydrates, Fats, and Proteins

Our next stop in exploring the physical properties of food is the aspect of food's chemical composition, which is the basis for food's classification as carbohydrates (including fiber), fats, and proteins.

Just as with calories, it is common practice to count grams of carbs, fiber, fats, and proteins to manage weight and health. Each food category has had its time in the spotlight either as a beneficial food or the one to blame for increasing statistics in the development of disease. Debates on what percentage of a diet should be carbohydrate versus protein versus fat is just that: a debate. Considering all of food's physical properties and viewing them through a holistic lens, we see that these percentages are variable and will change in a person through the ever-changing circumstances of his or her life.

First up are carbohydrates. Often misunderstood, carbohydrates are a vital part of any dietary pattern and indispensable to your well-being. Carbohydrates, in the form of the glucose stored in starch, deliver the sun's energy to fuel the body's activities and are the critical energy source for the brain and nerve tissue. There is a continuous need for glucose availability to the cells with minimal storage possibilities.

Having a steady availability of glucose allows the energy pathways in the body to function more efficiently. Without the presence of glucose, the body then relies on proteins from your lean tissue to keep the series of energy-extracting reactions working. The outcome is an altered metabolism and a body composition of less muscle, more fat.

Ever get moody when you've gone a long time without food? That is your signal that there's a need for carbohydrates to feed the brain. Carbohydrates are critical to your health. They play a role in cell-to-cell communication, regulate blood sugar levels through their fiber content, and maintain lean tissue while containing health-supportive compounds called *phytonutrients* that have anti-inflammatory and antioxidant protective properties. These critical roles are too often ignored because of the societal fear of carbohydrates and weight gain that has flooded mainstream trends and marketing in the food industry.

When speaking of carbohydrates, it is imperative to make clear what exactly fits under the term *carbohydrates*. Carbohydrates are whole foods that I can pick out of a tree, off a bush, or pull out of the ground. Think of them as foods designed by nature. These include fruits, vegetables, legumes, and grains. Bakery goods and mass-produced sweets are processed food, not carbohydrates, and belong in a completely different category: the processed food category. More than half the foods that are blamed for being bad carbohydrates also have a significant amount of fat in them, which took us on the fat-free craze—one reductionist and misleading stance after another.

Fiber is a component of carbohydrate foods. There are two different types of fiber: soluble and insoluble. Soluble fibers found in apples, barley, carrots, and lentils have demonstrated a delay in transit time through the digestive tract, resulting in regulation of blood glucose levels. Insoluble fiber, such as cellulose found in skins of fruit and starchy vegetables like corn, stimulate the gastrointestinal tract muscles to maintain their integrity and proper colon function.

Fiber-Rich Foods

- adzuki beans
- amaranth
- barley
- beet greens
- blueberries
- broccoli
- elderberries
- cauliflower
- chard
- collard greens
- green peas
- kale

- lentils
- mung beans
- oats
- pear
- pumpkin seeds

- raisins
- raspberries
- sweet potato
- winter squash
- black beans

Carbohydrates are also disease preventers. Free radical production, a result of energy metabolism, can lead to cell membrane and signaling impairment, inflamed connective tissues, and oxidized molecules impacting blood vessel integrity. The production of free radicals needs to be regulated by compounds called antioxidants, which come from phytonutrients found only in plants. With over a thousand phytonutrients identified, including categories of carotenoids, flavonoids, and polyphenols, it's time to redeem the carbohydrate and embrace its crucial role in promoting health and well-being.

Antioxidant-Rich Foods

- apricots
- almonds
- avocado
- beets
- berries
- broccoli
- brussels sprouts
- collard greens
- carrots

- garlic
- kale
- mustard greens
- papaya
- plums
- red grapes
- sweet potato
- turnip greens
- walnuts

Next up are the fats. Fats are another macronutrient of controversy, one that has hit the headlines with warnings about saturation content, promotion of margarine over butter, the fat-free craze, all the way up to the current healthy omega-3 fatty acid trend. But aside from all the marketing, fat is an essential part of your dietary pattern.

Although often correlated with disease and obesity, fat is a valuable nutrient playing important roles in energy production, cell membrane structure and communication, blood vessel contraction and dilation, and immune responses to inflammation and pain. Fats also provide the raw materials for compounds called prostaglandins that regulate and influence the function of all fifty trillion cells in your body. Psychologically, fats also promote a sense of satiety, giving a grounding effect and sense of security. Craving for fats is often related to the slowing-down effect they create.

You might have heard the latest buzz on omega-3 fatty acids (linolenic acid). These fatty acids, along with their counterpart omega-6 fatty acids (linoleic acid), work together, making not only their presence but the ratio between the two important to your health. Omega-6 fatty acids, found in vegetable oils, are easier to accumulate in the diet. Consider upping your omega-3 fatty acid foods from sources such as salmon, seaweeds, and walnuts to find a healthy balance between the two.

Understanding the full function of fats in the body lets you see this important food's ability to provide needed nourishment. Look past the obsession with weight management, seeing fat as the nemesis, and welcome all that fat truly represents. I know this may be difficult to accept, but eating fat is healthy and does not necessarily make you put on weight.

Omega-3 Rich Foods

- chia seeds
- collard greens
- flaxseeds
- halibut
- hemp seeds
- kidney beans
- navy beans
- pinto beans
- pumpkin seeds
- salmon
- sardines
- seaweeds
- soybeans
- walnuts

Finally, we have protein. Awarded a superior place in the nutrition world, protein is touted as the macronutrient for weight loss. This highly marketed association of protein to weight loss has made it difficult for people to appreciate protein's physiological roles within a well-balanced body dynamic. Protein supports the maintenance and growth of cells, assists in immune function, makes hormones, buffers the blood, maintains fluid and electrolyte balance, and provides the structure of tendons, ligaments, muscle fibers, and bone.

Protein is available through both animal and plant-based sources, making it a highly accessible nutrient. Debate and controversy continues over which source provides the most bioavailable protein, as researchers explore the biochemical impact of animal versus plant protein on inflammatory pathways. They also debate the advantages of grass-fed, pasture-raised animals versus those raised on factory farms, and complete plant protein concerns, including protein's front stage role in weight loss regimens showing up on bookshelves year after year. (This discussion will surface in the final stage of this journey as you explore the root chakra in stage 3.)

For now, it's important to understand that we can't deny that protein is an essential nutrient. It is only when protein is consumed in excess, particularly through animal sources, displacing other nutrients that an imbalance occurs.

The prevailing myth that animal sources are the only complete sources of protein, with vegans at risk for deficiency, needs to be retired. Nine out of the twenty amino acids (building blocks of protein) must come from your diet, since the body does not manufacture them. It has been said that plant-based foods do not contain all of these amino acids, making them inferior. The truth is plant sources such as in quinoa, soybean, buckwheat, hemp, pumpkin, and chia seeds do contain all nine essential amino acids, and they not only contain complete protein but are more bioavailable because of the array of additional nutrients within the food's innate design. The body is brilliant in that it does not require everything you need for health to come in each bite. The body has what's called an amino acid pool in cells and circulating in the blood, available to be synthesized into proteins as needed. Remember—your body's functions and health are impacted by your dietary pattern as a whole. Again, context matters.

Plant-Based Protein Foods

- almonds
- amaranth
- banana
- barley
- beets
- broccoli rabe
- buckwheat
- cashews
- cauliflower
- collard greens

- hemp seeds
- lentils
- millet
- navy beans
- soybeans
- split peas
- quinoa
- tempeh
- whole oats
- yams

Food for Thought

How do you categorize your food? Let's take a few examples. Lentils are commonly categorized as a carbohydrate, an incredible source of soluble and insoluble fiber. Lentils are also a high source of protein. So which camp do they go in? Carbohydrate? Protein? How about almonds? Almonds provide heart-healthy monounsaturated fats, fiber, and protein. Which camp do they belong in? And how about kale, squash, or brussels sprouts? All contain fiber, protein, and fatty acids.

The answer is to start talking *whole food*—not food divided into categories that are inaccurate and sometimes arbitrary. The nutrients in food are organized in combinations and patterns by nature for absorption and assimilation to occur. When we eat whole food, our bodies naturally metabolize the nutrients in that food needed at that moment. The "packaging" that these nutrients come in matters. Remember—the underlying design of the human being is one in which everything is linked and interconnected, so whole foods matter. I can't stress this concept enough; it's the key to shifting your entire relationship with food and has the potential to alter the way you live. It's that powerful!

Alkalinity of Foods

A third physical property of food is its ability to keep your blood oxygenated, supporting the body's ability to carry out its self-healing potential. When blood is overly acidic because of diet, it affects how your cells become oxygenated. Each cell requires oxygen to live. If cells are deprived of oxygen or limited because of red blood cells unable to deliver oxygen and nutrients to cells efficiently, the body's self-healing capacity begins to diminish.

Your food choices impact your blood's alkaline/acidic balance as measured by pH, a rating based on a scale of 0–14. Ideally, your blood is slightly alkaline, a range of 7.35–7.45, reflecting a state of optimal oxygenation. A pH in this range indicates you've got a strong line of defense against the growth of bacteria, yeast, fungus, and viruses. On the other hand, acidic blood will lead to compromised repair and maintenance of cells, alter detoxifying pathways, and disrupt organ function.

With the understanding that disease is created in an acidic environment, what choices can you make to help in maintaining your health? Along with the workings of your kidneys and lungs, your food choices play an important role. Consider eating a diet of primarily alkaline-forming foods. These foods create an alkaline ash after digestion, an effect not always revealed by the food's appearance on your plate. For example, lemons are acidic in nature but are alkaline forming within the body. Take a look at the chart below. This does not mean never eat acidic food or that acid-forming foods are bad for you. Avoid black-and-white thinking. It's always about balance and relationships.

Consider keeping your dietary pattern 70 percent alkaline and 30 percent acidic. This will ensure your body is working efficiently and is fully oxygenated, creating an uninhabitable home for bacteria and viruses while maintaining the circulation of blood and energy throughout your body.

Alkaline-Forming Foods	Acid-Forming Foods
fruits/vegetables	land animal protein
sea vegetables	milk/cheese
apple cider vinegar	white vinegar
flaxseed / olive oil / coconut oil	safflower oil / corn oil / peanut oil
sea salt / herbs / spices	beans
herbal teas / broth	alcohol / soft drinks
maple syrup / rice syrup	sugar/sweeteners
pumpkin seeds / almonds	pecans/walnuts
lentils/amaranth/millet/quinoa	wheat / barley / white flour

Epigenetics and Food

Continuing in our exploration of the full potential of the physical properties of food, we come to our fourth consideration, food's impact on our genes. Yes, your food choices can actually impact the expression of your genes.

Through a new branch of science called *epigenetics*, exciting answers on the topic are surfacing through the work of researchers like Bruce Lipton, who I mentioned earlier. Much advancement in the world of genetics can be traced back to the Human Genome Project in the 1990s, when a collaborative effort was made to isolate and map every human gene. The intention was to explore how genes control biology and to begin developing genetic methods to cure disease.

Researchers speculated that the human being had approximately 120,000 genes, yet by the completion of the project, it was discovered that the human body has approximately 25,000 genes—the same number as a rodent and about 1,000 more than a worm. It became clear that human's complexity came from other factors outside genes. That's when the science of epigenetics emerged. The current understanding is that genes, without altering the DNA blueprint, are expressed—turned on or off—in response to environmental signals that are either internal or external in nature.

This means that your genes do not turn on and off by themselves. Genes do not become active or dormant and just stay in that one position. The environment they are exposed to will continually determine their expression. Signals for gene expression include your thoughts, emotions, nutrition, lifestyle choices, and management of stress. These signals determine if and when a gene will become active or whether it will lie dormant regardless of its DNA sequence. So when you change the thoughts running through your head to ones of gratitude and joy and you choose foods that activate protective qualities in the body while making cancer cells dormant, you are altering the expression of your genes.

How amazing is that?

The genes you have are a static representation of what you could be. Take those genes and put them in an animated, living being, and they alter to become a unique representation of that person's life journey. No one, even if you are a twin, will have the same genetic expression as you, because your genetic expression is a reflection of your uniqueness. It is a cumulative depiction of all your thoughts, feelings, and lifestyle choices— your responses to the external world and its continuous life lessons, challenges, and gifts. And there is no one in the world like you. Your thoughts, dreams, wishes, fears, interests, and passions are completely your own.

Epigenetics is an eye-opening discovery for all of us. We had been told for so long that our health was predetermined by genes. We lived in a space where we accepted that our parents' and grandparents' fate would also be ours, regardless of what choices we might make. Whenever a client reaches out to address an illness, the statement "It runs in my family" is often in tow.

Yes, genes impact our health. But not as we once thought. Research studies are now demonstrating that at least 90 percent of illness is not a genetic inheritance. Illness is a complex interaction of countless variables.

How does this all translate into making the best food choices? Foods contain bioactive compounds that either directly or indirectly influence the expression of genes. Remember the health-promoting phytonutrients mentioned in the carbohydrates section earlier? Those plant-based compounds regulate gene function in positive ways, including silencing cancer cells. It is estimated that there are thousands of phytonutrients with protective and healing qualities found in the plants' pigment, flavor, vitamins, and even minerals, which is why plant-based diets are getting more widespread support.

Phytonutrients in Food

Phytonutrients	Food Sources
anthocyanins	blueberries, red cabbage, red grapes, pomegranates
betalains	beets, cactus pear, amaranth, rainbow chard
carotenoids	sweet potato, carrot, squash, apricot, tomato
catechins	broad beans, blackberries, green tea, apples
indoles	mustard greens, cabbage, cauliflower, kale, turnip
isoflavones	soybean, miso, tempeh
isothiocyanates	bok choy, brussels sprouts, kale, watercress
lignans	flaxseeds, sesame seeds, broccoli, cashews
lutein	broccoli, corn, snap peas, squash
phenolic acids	berries, mangos, plums, cherries
resveratrol	red grapes, blueberries, cranberries, peanuts
saponins	soybeans, navy beans, chickpeas, kidney beans
sulfides	garlic, onion, chives, leeks
zeaxanthin	spinach, kale, turnip greens, collard greens

One key factor in eating to support healthy gene expression is the requirement of a consistent dietary pattern, not an occasional apple or serving of broccoli. Genes continuously change their expression, remaining malleable and turning on and off depending on what you do. So it's not just your food choices in each moment that makes the difference, but rather making those choices on a consistent basis. It is your overall dietary pattern that will impact which genes are expressed and consequently the physical manifestation of health or disease.

CHAPTER 2

THE ENERGETIC POTENTIAL OF FOOD

After learning how food's physical characteristics can support our bodies' capacity to heal and meet our health goals, you can go deeper to explore the subtle underlying energy of food. In order to grasp food's full potential, it is important to add the energetic, intangible aspect of food into the equation. It's here where the hidden messages of food start to be revealed.

If you remain aware only of the physical properties, your potential for long-term health, vitality, and weight loss will be a constant struggle. The energetic domain is where you can learn to powerfully personalize your dietary pattern and begin the exploration to discover your authentic self.

Let's begin with an overview of the ancient teachings of Traditional Chinese Medicine to understand the gift of life—your *qi*, or life force.

Traditional Chinese Medicine (TCM)

The ancient teachings of Traditional Chinese Medicine were recorded in a text now translated and found in *The Yellow Emperor's Classic of Medicine*. Within this text's pages and practiced for thousands of years is the belief that food synergistically holds an energetic vibration and flavor that impacts your overall well-being. It is possible to merge this ancient wisdom into the modern world to assist in preventive care and treatment, going so far as to be the platform of personal growth and evolution. This is exactly the intention behind *The Hidden Messages in Food*.

TCM tells us that we have a universal energy running through us, animating us and giving us the gift of life. This universal energy is made up of two primary and opposite forces called the yin and the yang. The two polarities are in constant flux, and their connection with each other is what determines the nature of the universe.

Everything comes down to relationships. The yang force is active and reflects expansion, movement, and growth. The yin force is passive, demonstrating the art of receptivity, contraction, and stability. The relationship and interaction of these two polarities manifests into five elements that exist in all matter: Water, Wood, Fire, Earth, and Metal.

Each one of us has unique combination of these elements, making up what is called our energetic constitution. We can be viewed holistically as having an energetic constitution, a biological DNA blueprint, and a nonmaterial soul—all at once. Through the holistic paradigm, all aspects are welcomed into the equation, creating a bigger picture where our awareness expands toward greater wholeness. You will be introduced to the general concepts of TCM in stage 2, "Eating in Sync with the Seasons," and then begin to use nature as a continual guide on your journey.

Getting back to the yin and the yang, we see that foods take on the qualities of one or the other of these two polarities. This occurs through food's systemic effects on the body through body temperature, qi (life force energy) movement, and the stimulation of specific energy meridians and organs through distinct flavors of food.

Thermal Nature

Each food has a thermal nature, or a post-digestion temperature, that affects your body's thermostat. Some foods have a warming or cooling nature, regardless of whether they are consumed raw or cooked; rather, it is part of their essence. There are also foods that have a more neutral nature, making little impact on the body's temperature.

Warming foods bring your energy and blood up and out to the surface of the body, moving qi and improving blood circulation. Cooling foods pull energy in and down, lowering the body's temperature. As you become more aware, you can choose foods that keep you aligned with your current needs. If you are experiencing cold hands or feet, or the winter season's chill, consuming warming foods can assist in bringing back balance within. If you are experiencing an internal heat or a hot summer's day, your food choices might shift to more cooling foods to complement your needs. The body is constantly swinging its pendulum between the polarities of yin and yang, contractive and expansive, seeking a balanced or homeostatic nature.

Thermal Nature of Foods

Warming	Neutral	Cooling
oats	pineapple	avocado
quinoa	sweet potato	mango
black beans	adzuki beans	peaches
tempeh	beets	amaranth
kale	carrot	mung beans
mustard greens	cabbage	seaweed
fennel	cashews	watercress
onion	brown rice	cucumber
garlic	buckwheat	sprouts
root vegetables	lentils	citrus

Moving Qi and Nourishing Organs

In addition to having an impact on your body's thermostat, your food choices can play a role in circulating qi and nourishing your organs.

One way to nourish your organs is through the flavors of different foods. But be careful—make sure not to associate flavor with taste. Taste is a combination of your taste bud receptors in your mouth, the entire gastrointestinal tract, as well as olfactory receptors that detect scents and odors. Just think of those times when you are congested and can't *taste* your food. Flavor is an intrinsic quality that may or may not align with its taste.

The salty flavor has a cooling and moistening nature, nourishing the kidneys while providing a grounding effect. Sour has a contracting and astringent effect, stimulating the liver and assisting in detoxification processes. Bitter foods are contracting and cooling, clearing away heat and penetrating the heart. The sweet flavor is linked to the central Earth element, creating a harmonizing and relaxing effect. The pungent flavor is expansive and dispersive, clearing the lungs and stimulating energy and blood circulation.

Furthermore, each flavor correlates to one of the five elements in nature's seasons and will also play a role in nourishing your chakras, or energy centers, something you will learn more about in stages 2 and 3 of your journey.

Flavors				
Sour	**Bitter**	**Sweet**	**Pungent**	**Salty**
lemons	rye	fig	scallions	sea salt
limes	celery	beets	ginger	seaweed
vinegar	quinoa	almonds	garlic	barley
grapes	asparagus	squash	leeks	millet
raspberries	arugula	mushrooms	fennel	kelp
mango	dandelion	meat	basil	miso
plum	parsley	soybeans	peppermint	oysters
papaya	citrus peel	buckwheat	cloves	clams
apple	mustard	eggs	rosemary	sardines

Vibrational Essence of Foods

People who eat animal foods often keep their distance from the piece of meat sitting on the plate. When I introduce the idea that how an animal is raised makes a difference, a student is often quick to put up their hand and say, "Stop. Don't tell me. I don't want to know—it will ruin eating meat for me." It's amazing how we can be so disconnected from the food we are eating, wanting to see animal food only as a bunch of calories or slab of protein on the plate.

The truth is all of it is energy. Humans, animals, and plants are all forms of energy. Just as our human bio-field (or *aura*, in energetic terms) is composed of our thoughts and feelings, the bio-field of an animal also carries the innate nature of its species and impressions of the life it has lived. Therefore, when you eat an animal, their vibration as well as their physical food properties will interact with yours.

As we arrive at the root chakra in stage 3, you will see where this helps reveal another dimension of you.

Colors of Food

There's more to the color of food and the appealing presentation it may give your meals than meets the eye. Colors have a vibrational frequency that resonates with your own energetic being, drawing to you particular foods of different colors. In stage 3, you will learn how the foods you gravitate toward or dislike and their colors deliver messages, telling you what aspects of your life may seek nourishment and healing. Simply observing the colors you are drawn to or have an aversion to can be a starting point in understanding the direction and health needs of your current life.

For some time, I became a lover of the color blue, which was apparent in my wardrobe that on any day was some shade of blue. I also recognized my disgust for anything red. We all can become quite passionate about our colors—something that always makes me smile. For some, liking or disliking a color doesn't go beyond it being a preference in clothing or linens. But within the holistic paradigm, this information actually means something more. During my blue-color days, it meant that lessons in decision-making and finding my center were summoning my attention. We attract into our lives the things we need to learn. You will soon see where your favorite colors are leading you.

CHAPTER 3

A HOLISTIC APPROACH TO MEALTIME

Having come to a fuller understanding of food and its potential to impact your life holistically, you are now ready for the final step in stage 1. Applying your new awareness of the physical and energetic properties of food, mealtime becomes an adventure in preparing food and creating the environment that includes your body, mind, and soul.

As explained at the beginning of stage 1, the value of food comes not only from what is being eaten but also from the variables within each person who is eating it. Once the full picture of food is seen in this more personalized context, healthy eating requires asking three questions of any meal to round out the full potential of food: What is the source of the food? How is it prepared? In what environment is the meal eaten? In this chapter, you will explore these questions and have a chance to apply all you've learned so far to your mealtime experience.

Source of the Food

Is the food you eat from local farms or from supermarkets supplied by mass producers? As already discussed, how food is grown and harvested and the living conditions of the animals you are eating makes a tremendous difference in the energetic and physical value of the food.

An important topic to consider is whether the food is organic versus conventional. The label "certified organic" on plant food means crops are free of synthetic pesticides, sewage-based fertilizers, ripening chemicals, and genetically modified organisms (GMOs). Organic livestock have access to the outdoors and sunlight and are raised without use of antibiotics, growth hormones, or diets of animal byproducts. A discussion of organic versus conventional food can become an entire book in itself, with points being made from the perspectives of health advocates, environmental agencies, food distributors, scientists and researchers, and even the biotech industry.

There will continue to be debates on what is considered healthy, loosely defining the phrase "safe for consumption," especially with the growing use of GMOs. There's evidence of elevated immune responses in individuals with the change in food production methods; however, lifetime studies are not available, and the unreliable methodology of epidemiological nutrition studies is another debate.

What we do know is crops and animals grown or raised in the most natural conditions deliver food that has the least allergens, chemicals, and hormones and has the highest energetic vibration. With the rise in immune-based illness and inflammatory conditions in society, this can be a great motivator to choose organic. Each time you do, it's not just for you and your family. You are part of a bigger movement of change, persuading more farmers to choose organic farming conditions.

Preparing Your Food

How food is prepared impacts the bioavailability of nutrients along with the energetic vibration that interacts with your unique bio-field. You have options of poaching, steaming, pressure cooking, braising, baking, and frying. Each cooking method impacts the bioavailability and integrity of the food's constituents.

Some foods require heat versus being consumed raw in order to make nutrients active, especially the health-promoting phytonutrients found in plants. Heat breaks down a plant's cell walls and makes nutrients residing in the cell walls available for absorption in the body. Lycopene, the red pigment in tomatoes and red bell peppers, known for its antioxidant and cancer-fighting properties, increases when heated. Not only do cooked carrots release more carotenoids, or immune-boosting antioxidants, but absorption increases in the presence of fat.

Some greens, such as spinach, chard, and beet greens, contain oxalic acid. When eaten raw, this acid interferes with mineral absorption, stopping essential minerals such as calcium, magnesium, iron, zinc, and copper from being absorbed in the intestines. A quick application of heat—wilting the greens in a quick sauté or adding to a soup in the last minute of cooking—will break down the oxalic acid and make the minerals more available.

Does this mean you should never eat raw tomatoes, carrots, or spinach? No! That would be more of the black-and-white thinking I'm trying to steer you away from. Cooking is an essential path to long-term digestive and immune health, so it should never be a black-and-white situation. *Nothing* ever is!

The application of heat does not always give a desirable effect, especially when it comes to cooking with fats. How fats are processed and used in preparation impacts the fat's innate health-promoting qualities. Terms such as *hydrogenation* and *trans-fatty acid* have flooded the advertising campaigns of major food producers. Hydrogenation is a process where unsaturated fats are placed under high heat to transfigure the fats for a longer shelf life. Unfortunately, during the process, the beneficial characteristics are destroyed as the unsaturated fat is converted into a saturated fat. Through hydrogenation, not only can the physical properties and degree of saturation be altered, but the fatty acids can also change their shape, resulting in a fat with detrimental effects to the body's functioning. Trans fats lead to inflammation, decreased insulin responses, altered energy metabolism, and increased risk of cardiovascular disease.

When does hydrogenation and trans fats happen? Let's look at cooking temperatures. Chemistry reveals hydrogenation to occur at 302°F, trans-fatty acids begin developing at 320°F, and the refinement process of the food industry occurs at 450°F. What does that say about the majority of processed foods and the food preparation temperatures you may choose to cook at? It's a clear indication that the fats and oils are rancid and toxic. Remember the hydrogenation process not only alters the physical structure and properties of the unsaturated fats but also depletes the oil of the majority of vitamins, minerals, and essential fatty acids it once contained.

The good thing is that poaching, steaming, simmering, braising, pressure cooking, sautéing, and baking all can happen below the high temperatures that alter the integrity of fats. This may just require you to expand your cooking methods, which is never a bad thing.

This does not mean to completely omit saturated fats from your dietary pattern, however. Clarified butter, also known as *ghee*, has a strong presence in traditional East Indian teachings of Ayurveda and is a unique saturated butter that has been known for its immune-boosting effects and promotion of digestive health through the presence of butyric acid, conjugated linoleic acid, and fat-soluble vitamins A, D, E, and K. This saturated fat, which can withstand high temperatures and still hold its health benefit, cannot be overlooked or marked with the "saturated fat equals bad" stamp.

Coconut oil, another saturated fat, strengthens our immune system with additional antiviral and antimicrobial benefits through its compounds of lauric acid, capric acid, caprylic acid, and polyphenols. Perhaps when high heat is required for cooking preparation, clarified butter or coconut oil can be used, reserving more delicate oils for low heat to raw preparation needs. There are so many variables to food and its preparation. This is why it is so important to see each food trait as being in context to the whole experience.

The Eating Environment

After considering food's sources and preparation, let's explore the actual dining experience. What kind of environment do you choose to dine in? Everything about the atmosphere that you are eating in impacts how nutrients are assimilated and the energetic healing abilities within your food.

First, become more aware of the physical environment you are eating in. There's a difference between eating on the go or standing at the counter while surfing the internet and dining in a relaxed atmosphere, seated, with no time restraints, and in the company of those you enjoy. The digestive process requires appropriate chewing, not a bite-swallow method, along with time for the body to communicate feelings of satiety. When you eat your meal in five minutes, your brain has no chance to send signals of fullness that on average take fifteen minutes. Do your digestion a favor and *slow down*!

Food does more than feed your grumbling stomach—it nourishes all of you, body, mind, and soul. This is one reason the Mediterranean diet is touted as being among the healthiest. Certainly olive oil in the Mediterranean diet has benefits, along with a greater abundance of fresh vegetables and fish in the dietary pattern as compared to American diets, but that's not the whole of it. Mediterranean people sit down to eat as if every meal were an important social event. There is no rushing through the meal; instead eating is a mindful experience, full of conversation and laughter. When family and friends are gathered, the energetic vibration is often the highest possible—love.

Be aware of your state of mind as you sit down to dine. When you are upset or in a rush, this impacts food assimilation all the way to the cellular level. How you feel, along with the person who prepared the food and those you are sharing the meal with, impacts the assimilation of your food.

Watch your beliefs about the meal in front of you. Do you find yourself saying, "Oh, this meal is so bad for me! I'm definitely gaining weight after eating this!"? Guess what? You probably will! Those thoughts and their associated emotions of guilt or shame elicit a physiological response in the body. Food reacts differently within the body simply based on whether you believe the food is bad for you versus believing it is a form of nourishment. That is how powerful your thoughts and beliefs are!

Have you ever had a meal that was spectacular and then when you went to have it again, the taste wasn't even close? The same exact recipe and ingredients were used. The environment, all the way to the energetic vibration of the cook, is in that meal! That's why growing up I loved my mom's chicken cutlets and would not eat them anywhere else. She didn't do anything fancy to them. There was no secret culinary technique. She made them with the vibration of love. Love, the highest vibration, alters the food. Again, food is more than nutrients; it is nourishment for your body, mind, and soul.

Remember—everything is energy, with all vibrations interacting. What does this mean practically? A few basic guidelines: Do not eat when you are angry or upset. If you feel an unsettling vibe as you enter a restaurant, go somewhere else to eat. Most of all, eat with people whose company you truly enjoy. Do not eat with people you do not get along with, because it can disrupt your digestive system and the ability to extract nutrients. The atmosphere that you eat in is so important that I would rather you eat fast food in the company of someone you adore than eat your bowl of steamed vegetables while sitting silently across from someone who makes you boil.

Daily Self-Assessment Tool

As you move between stage 1 and stage 2, begin to incorporate the following self-assessment tool to help you bring the full potential of food, both physical and energetic, into your food and meal choices. It all begins simply with awareness. With each stage, I will add a few more questions to the list. By the time you finish stage 3, you will have a complete tool to use in making sure that you are getting the full hidden messages in food.

In stage 1, the purpose of this assessment is to help you become consistent in your awareness of what's happening for you. Use it as a scan to do daily, and over time it will happen more quickly, literally in under a minute. In the beginning, like anything new, it may take longer. Perhaps you haven't been in the habit of spending time connecting to your body or engaged in this type of contemplation with yourself. But that's the point—it's time to start!

Again, it is important to take this time, one to ten minutes, for yourself to check in. You are worth it!

Stage 1 Self-Assessment Tool

1. Overall, how are you feeling (present, relaxed, calm, distracted, anxious, annoyed, or other)?
2. How are your energy levels (ready to go, light and alert, tired, heaviness in body, or other)?
3. Are you feeling internally hot or cold? How do your hands and feet feel?
4. Are you hydrated?

5. How are your bowel movements (diarrhea, constipated, daily frequency, or other)?
6. Do you feel dry (skin, throat, digestive system), or do you feel damp (bloated, swelling, congested)?
7. Was your diet in the past day more alkaline or acidic?
8. Have your recent meal choices been more whole foods or more processed foods?
9. Are you eating a lot of animal products? Any particular ones?
10. What kind of environment are you eating your meals in (peaceful, disruptive, with company, alone, or other)?

STAGE 2

EATING IN SYNC WITH THE SEASONS

In stage 1 of your transformative journey, you learned to approach food holistically by seeing food's true potential for your health, both physically and energetically. This new awareness shifts the perspective from seeing eating as a purely mechanical process to an activity that is intelligent and purposeful. In stage 2, we will add another layer of seeing through the holistic lens to connect you and your food choices to the greater natural world. Here you will see how the rhythm and forces of nature influence your health through the changing seasons and how eating in sync with the seasons can bring you into a deeper relationship with the foods you choose.

CHAPTER 4

EMBRACING NATURE'S RHYTHMS

The holistic paradigm is about wholeness, synergy, patterns, and relationships, best described as *interconnectivity*. Interconnectivity applies to all of life, from elements of nature to the seasons and climate, from food provided by Mother Earth to the workings of the human body. It means there is a constant merging and interaction within the parts of each of these, but also an exchange with one another. In this view, you see each aspect as not only a whole within itself but also a part of something bigger. I use the term *Universe* to refer to this bigger picture, emphasizing the interconnectivity of the holistic paradigm as encompassing all of it.

According to the Eastern view, we as humans are miniature versions of the greater picture, the Universe. Everything that is found in the universe is also found within us. This is illustrated through the cyclical pattern of the five element theory of Traditional Chinese Medicine, demonstrating how each elemental aspect in nature—Water, Wood, Fire, Earth, and Metal—creates, transforms, and nourishes the others.

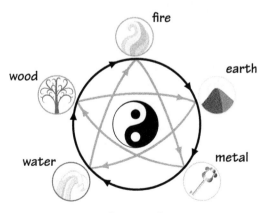

Five Element Theory

An example that everyone can relate to is the weather. The day can feel cold and dry, just as you can feel an internal dryness accompanied by a constant chill and cold hands or feet. There are days when the sky is clear and bright, and your mind can be clear and light. There are also cloudy, gloomy days that you can feel within, making you want to curl up on the sofa with a blanket. How often have you heard or even said to yourself, when feeling bodily aches and pains, that it must be the change in weather? *My knees knew two days ago that it was going to rain.* Does that sound familiar? You are that connected to nature.

When you begin to see yourself as a miniature version of the universe with everything in nature also existing inside you, a new awareness of your nutritional needs follows. As you observe the seasons, you begin to make food choices to live in harmony with nature and create a path to find your own more expanded human nature.

As we explore the seasons and their transitional phases, you will see how each of the five elements of nature is aligned with a specific season, that season's essence and personal traits, physical organs, climate, and food and flavor recommendations. Regardless of whether where you live has an outside temperature that changes drastically or remains relatively the same throughout the year, these elemental phases of the seasons still occur. The holistic nature and shifting of the Universe's energy may not be as apparent, but they are still occurring behind the scenes and influencing your health and well-being.

The Wood Element: Spring

Wood symbolizes creation and new beginnings. Trees represent the Wood element, demonstrating the firmness or deep connection to the Earth and the flexibility of the tree itself to adapt to nature's changes. You are like a tree in that you are designed to grow, adapt, and transform within your existing environment.

WOOD ELEMENT

Season: Spring
Essence: Creation
Organs: Liver/Gall Bladder
Climate: Wind
Flavor: Sour

Essence and Personal Traits. In the Wood phase, you start to become conscious of your unique self. This is the beginning of an inner reliance and knowing through which you will define yourself outside of family or societal roles. When Wood is balanced within, you are bold, ambitious, and have the courage to act in your own best interests.

When out of balance, you become inflexible in all domains—body, mind, and soul. This inflexibility can manifest as inflammation in tendons or in a rigid mindset. You may find yourself short-tempered and impatient as the emotion of anger surfaces. Obstruction or resistance to Wood's essence of renewal and moving forward can manifest through aggressive behavior, or you might swing to the other side with a more passive, indecisive nature.

When I consciously watch my behavior during the spring season, I can recognize how my threshold for patience can lower and my responses to others may be conveyed as insensitive and sometimes even with a harsh tone. I notice that I may also raise my voice. Although my assertive and driven qualities make it possible for me to continuously create and envision new plans, when my Wood energy is out of balance, it takes on an exaggerated nature.

Physical Organs. The energy pattern of Wood is linked to the organs of liver and gallbladder. The liver has the role of distributing and maintaining a smooth, uninterrupted flow of qi, blood, and even emotions throughout the body. The liver plays a major role in the detoxifying process and maintaining immunity. The gallbladder assists in fat digestion and also metaphorically represents choice and decision-making. When the liver and gallbladder are not functioning efficiently, stagnation arises, disrupting the essence of the Wood phase, which is renewal, flexibility, and feelings of ease and harmony. Holistically, organs are more than anatomical structures comprised of physiological functions. They are connected to the intangible domains of emotion, mind, and spirit.

Climate. The Wood element is associated with the climate of wind. Wind can come either as a penetrating force or a gently soothing breeze. It clears out the old and makes room for the new—new thoughts, ideas, people, circumstances, adventures. Wind is an agent of change. This is what the spring season is all about. We've all experienced that feeling of a fresh new start and energy of inspiration after a long, cold winter as everything in nature starts to bud and surface.

The energy in the spring is rising and expanding. At this time, the liver is its most sensitive, a perfect opportunity to begin cleansing or "spring-cleaning." This cleansing need not be a fast, but instead an opportunity to reset the body and remove toxins, creating a strengthened and renewed inner environment. We are bringing movement into our beings.

Any cleansing program must focus on the liver. The most metabolically active organ in the body performing over five hundred functions, the liver is one of the main organs responsible for detoxification. Secondary organs are the lungs, digestive tract, kidneys, skin, and connective tissue. The liver has been referred to as a clearinghouse for its role in recycling, regenerating, and detoxifying our tissues.

You are exposed to toxins from the external environment as well as internal environment called exotoxins and endotoxins, respectively. This list can include air pollution, food additives and preservatives, hormone-raised animal foods, and repressed emotions as well as the effects of metabolism in the body and the simple act of breathing. The liver reformats these toxins, making them harmless and ready for elimination from the body, a process called conjugation. But conjugation requires the help of certain nutrients to be effective, underscoring the food recommendations for the spring season.

Food Recommendations. Eating for the spring season, with the intention of a new start and a regeneration of your being, requires emphasizing the plant kingdom in your food choices.

There are several reasons why you'd want to eat a more plant-based diet in the spring. Plants are foods with natural detoxifying properties, they take an anti-inflammatory pathway within the body, and they have an alkaline-forming effect on the blood. Ultimately, plant-based foods aid in regeneration of the body's functioning.

The characteristics of food previously discussed in stage 1, including alkalinity, epigenetics, carbohydrates, and flavors and colors of food also come into play. Plant-based foods are rich sources of phytonutrients, the health-promoting chemicals that assist in nourishing the liver, stimulating the circulation of qi and blood, and strengthening your body's reserves and metabolic processes.

Cruciferous vegetables become a major player in the dietary pattern at this time. This includes arugula, bok choy, watercress, collard greens, cauliflower, kale, and brussels sprouts.

When preparing your meals, especially during a time of detoxification and renewal, it is best to lightly cook your foods. You are coming out of a winter, so a transition is happening, which means the winter's needs are still being nurtured in the early weeks of spring. It's a gradual shift, not the flick of a light switch. Eating cooked food versus raw will assist in digestive function, bioavailability of nutrients, and the continued detoxification process. Light cooking, even a forty-five-second blanching, will work as will a steam, simmer, bake, or sauté.

Along with a dietary pattern emphasizing cruciferous vegetables, pack your meals with plenty of leafy greens—the more bitter the better. First, greens are loaded with chlorophyll, the green pigment that oxygenates your cells, and second, their bitter flavor promotes the liver's cleansing and detoxification processes. The body is a self-healing entity with every cell going through a life cycle. It continually repairs, renews, and regenerates all the way down to the cellular level. The spring season is a heightened time for this process.

Flavors. In regard to flavor, sour is the dominant flavor of Wood but by no means to the exclusion of other flavors. Remember everything is connected. Sour foods directly stimulate energy flow to the liver and gallbladder. They have a contracting and astringent effect aiding in digestion and the liver's detoxification.

It doesn't require an abundance of sour flavor to aid the liver. Drinking warm lemon water to begin the day with the additions of apple cider vinegar and raw sauerkraut to your daily dietary pattern will do the trick.

General Recommendations. Allow your diet to become lighter as you eliminate rich, fatty, and all processed foods. Look around the produce section of your grocery store with a keener eye, as fresh food will be arriving in abundance. Meal portions will begin to grow smaller. You are coming out of the winter slumber, no longer hibernating and eating heavy meals. With new beginnings, it's time to move.

Remember Wood dislikes stagnation. Imagine a stagnant pond. This is not the ideal environment for renewal, healing, and longevity. Get your blood and qi flowing, and as you overcome inertia, start planning what you are going to create in your life in the coming year. This is a season to plan and strategize, but playfully.

Spring Eating Strategies

- Emphasize a plant-based diet.
- Incorporate cruciferous vegetables into your daily meals.
- Load up on the bitter, leafy greens.
- Include foods of the sour flavor daily.
- Eat most meals cooked versus raw.
- Cooking preparations include blanch, steam, simmer, sauté, and bake.
- Eliminate rich, fatty, and processed foods.
- Stay hydrated.
- Add garlic, scallions, and ginger if your seasonal allergies kick in.
- Decrease your food portions and start exercising.

The Fire Element: Summer

While the Wood phase stressed individuation and initiating movement, as you enter into the Fire phase, correlated to the season of summer, you begin to engage others.

FIRE ELEMENT

Season: Summer
Essence: Transformation
Organs: Heart/Small Intestines
Climate: Hot
Flavor: Bitter

Essence and Personal Traits. Fire represents transformation and the action that will manifest the plans you created during the spring. At this time, nature is at its peak, rife with flowers in bloom and trees bearing fruit. The summer is a time of expansion, full of light and heat.

When your Fire element is balanced, you are full of energy, passion, and enthusiasm. You are social and enjoy interacting with others, open to activity and adventure. When your Fire element is out of balance, you try too hard to connect with others, becoming eager to please and displaying a clingy nature with underlying anxiety.

Physical Organs. The Fire phase is associated with the heart, the small intestines, the triple heater meridian (acupuncture point associated with the heart), and pericardium (sac containing the heart). The heart is so much more than a mechanical pump. It is an intelligence system with its own electromagnetic force containing its own nervous system and hormone-producing abilities. In TCM, it is the center of emotions and known as the home of spirit connecting us to the Universe. The heart's vibrational frequencies allow for an exchange of energy between heart and brain in the individual, as well as between self and others nearby.

The heart is considered the emperor of all other organs as it structurally governs the blood vessels and the body's nourishment. In TCM, it is considered the seat of consciousness, housing your soul and responsible for internal harmony. The small intestines assist in the digestive processes by separating the food to assimilate from the by-products to be excreted. The small intestines are physiologically separating the pure from the impure in food terms and energetically filtering outdated thoughts, beliefs, and emotions no longer serving you. The triple heater meridian is part of TCM's heating and cooling system that is also connected to the energetic vibration in the outer environment. The pericardium acts as an outer heart protector, energetically monitoring the emotional trustworthiness of others and determining your openness or degree of vulnerability in any circumstance.

Climate. Summer can bring on a hot climate. This is the season when raw foods are most beneficial, depending on the individual and climate temperature.

If you find yourself with a strong internal fire, you may benefit from adding raw foods into your dietary pattern but not to the exclusion of cooked options. Invite quick-cooking techniques such as blanching, stir-fry, grill, or sautéing into your culinary repertoire during the summer season. Eating more in alignment with the Fire element in summer is a way to connect with others, nurture your Fire element, and boost your heart's vitality, making socializing without excessive attachment possible.

Food Recommendations. Eating for the Fire phase and season of summer requires keeping it bright and light. When choosing foods, those with a cooling thermal nature are most beneficial. This resembles a *rainbow diet*, full of fruits and vegetables with minimal meats, eggs, nuts, and oils. Animal-based or rich foods all create internal heat, and this is a time to cool. Grilling chicken and burgers, a favorite American fare, are actually thermally hot and not necessarily aligned with Fire needs. Those foods will become more appropriate as the seasons shift toward the seasons of autumn and winter.

At this time of year, meals are the lightest, full of vibrant colors and continuing the emphasis on the plant kingdom. Consider the largest meal of the day at lunchtime when your digestive fire is the highest. Keep thinking rainbow diet. Cool and hydrate through watery fruits, such as watermelon and cantaloupe. Seek out the stone fruits, such as peaches, apricots, nectarines, plums, and cherries. I am all smiles when the pluots (hybrid of an apricot and plum) make their way to the market! Go ahead and add beans with an innate cooling nature, such as mung, soybean, and navy beans. Sprouted beans are an even better choice.

Flavor. Foods with a bitter flavor are the essential flavor of this season, with contracting and cooling qualities to penetrate the heart and support the liver. This includes dandelion greens, lacinato kale, endive, escarole, chard, asparagus, celery, and the alkaline grains amaranth and quinoa.

General Recommendations. In this season, consider preparing more meals with family and friends. It's no surprise that summer is a great time for a barbecue. Sunshine, cooking together, and the enjoyment of lawn games fulfills Fire's requirement for social interaction and companionship.

Summer Eating Strategies

- Continue to emphasize a plant-based dietary pattern.
- Meals are the lightest and brightest of the year.
- Eat a rainbow diet.
- Keep the bitter flavor dominant.
- Incorporate foods with a cooling nature.
- Cooking preparations include raw, blanch, stir-fry, grill, and sauté.
- Hydrate through drinking and high-water-content fruits.
- Add stone fruits to your diet.
- Eat your largest meal at lunchtime.
- Take your dining experiences outside, and enjoy the company of friends and family.

The Earth Element: Transition between Seasons

Fire turns to ash and brings us to the Earth phase, the primary stabilizing and centering force for transitioning between the seasons and between all of the other four elements.

EARTH ELEMENT

Season: Transitions
Essence: Grounding
Organs: Stomach/Spleen
Climate: Dampness
Flavor: Sweet

Essence and Personal Traits. The Earth element is present at the end of summer and in times of any seasonal transition. The Earth has been referred to as the mother or nurturer of life, continuously giving of herself. Being the centering element, Earth represents a grounding sense of belonging that anchors us to the physical world.

When you feel centered and grounded, there is a sense of security that allows you to step out of your routine world and live expansively. Earth represents concepts of home and our exchange with the outside world as well as the integration of mind and body or left and right brain hemispheres. When your Earth element is balanced, you are sympathetic, patient, and have a strong sense of self with defined boundaries. When out of balance, you may find yourself meddlesome and smothering in an attempt to feel connected.

Physical Organs. The spleen and stomach are the organs of this centering element. The health of these organs is essential not only to digestive health but to your overall vitality. With digestive organs playing a dominant role during the shift in seasons, it is important to place more attention on how you are eating during those times.

Digestion is about movement and transformation, and digestive processes are warm transactions that require food to reach a temperature slightly higher than core body temperature for effective transformation of nutrients to occur. This means the food needs to become a soup in your stomach. A great analogy by Bob Flaws in his book *Tao of Healthy Eating* is looking at the stomach as a pot on the stove and the spleen as the fire underneath it. For digestion to occur, which is a process of assimilation and separation of pure versus impure, the temperature of the process needs to be a little warmer than core temperature.

Continue to think warm transactions when seeking to align with the Earth element. Remaining with the above analogy, if there were a flame beneath a pot on the stove (in this case, the flame is the spleen), water or dampness would inhibit the spleen's function by dousing out the flame. Cooked food can be viewed as a form of predigested food, providing a warm and appropriate environment to break down and distill the food while separating the nutrients for absorption from the by-products for elimination.

Climate. The climate of the Earth element is one of dampness. In the digestive process, foods influence the amount of fluids your body produces, referred to in Eastern teachings as dampness. The question becomes, how damp is the food you are eating? If the food is excessively damp, the functions of the stomach and spleen are compromised, leading to stagnant blood and qi flow with the development of mucous and phlegm. The goal is to create a balance.

Food Recommendations. While choosing a dietary pattern of cooked foods to nourish the Earth element in times of transition, consider making an effort to eat *prebiotic* foods. Prebiotic foods contain fibrous compounds that pass through the small intestines undigested and stimulate the growth of friendly gut bacteria. This bacterial environment known as your *microbiome* is essential to intestinal health, the absorption of minerals, blood sugar regulation, and decreasing inflammatory responses. The two most understood prebiotic fibers are inulin and fructooligosaccharides. High prebiotic sources include garlic, onions, leeks, Jerusalem artichokes, dandelion greens, bananas, beets, fennel, lentils, and cabbage. Eating prebiotic foods is an overall dietary recommendation yet with a higher emphasis during times of transition in seasons.

Probiotic foods are fermented foods that already contain live microbes to assist in balancing your gut flora. You may have noticed the rise in availability of foods such as kimchee, sauerkraut, miso, and tempeh—all of which are probiotics.

Flavor. The essential flavor of the Earth element is sweet. Dampening foods contain sweetness, becoming excessive in juices, sugars, wheat, nuts, eggs, dairy, meat, alcohol, and processed or fried foods. There are foods that are sweet without excess dampness, such as beets, squash, carrots, mushrooms, sweet potatoes, pears, apples, or coconut.

When reviewing your food journal, don't be surprised if most of your food choices are on the dampening list. It's a common occurrence. Keep in mind that prior to refrigeration, only one hundred years ago, drinking concentrated juices and eating animal flesh were not part of the daily diet. One hundred years is not long enough for the body to evolve and adapt to such a shift in diet. Excess dampness can surface in different ways, such as a struggle with weight management, chronic sinus infections, respiratory issues, sugar imbalances, lack of energy, inability to concentrate, and excessive worry. Too much dampness in the body can make you feel heavy, literally pulling you down to the Earth for stability or grounding.

General Recommendations. You may have become accustomed to chilled and cold foods in your dietary pattern, including a glass of iced tea, ice cream, freshly squeezed orange juice, and the morning vegetable smoothie. In reference to the stomach and spleen, cold and raw foods impede the digestive processes because of cold negating heat and water putting out fire. If your intention is to nurture your Earth element and strengthen your digestive system, then raw and chilled foods may not be the best choices.

Make a conscious effort to shift to cooked foods for the few weeks surrounding the change in each season and eat less raw food in general. Steaming, poaching, simmering, and some stewing are ideal at these times. With these changes, observe if you experience improved digestion, clear sinuses, more energy, and even a more centered feeling in your everyday affairs.

Eating Strategies for Transitioning the Seasons

- Emphasize plant-based dietary pattern.
- Eat all meals cooked during the shift in seasons.
- Incorporate the sweet flavor through vegetables, grains, and dense fruits.
- Avoid damp forming foods during times of transition: sugar, meat, dairy, and wheat.
- Increase prebiotic foods to feed friendly gut bacteria.
- Add probiotic foods such as kimchee, sauerkraut, or tempeh.
- Bring soups into your daily regimen.
- Cooking preparations include steam, simmer, poach, and stew.
- Include digestive spices in cooking: cardamom, ginger, caraway, and fennel.
- Spend time in nature—go barefoot if possible.

The Metal Element: Autumn

The Metal phase marks a time of preparation when we begin to gather and store energy for the coming winter months. The leaves have fallen, and tree sap is moving downward into the roots while squirrels begin to fatten up, grow a thicker coat, and bury nuts in preparation for the cold winter. It is our time, too, to turn inward and do less physical activity as we make more nurturing and supportive choices in diet and activity.

METAL ELEMENT

Season: Autumn
Essence: Authenticity
Organs: Lung/Large Intestines
Climate: Dry
Flavor: Pungent

Essence and Personal Traits. The element of Metal signifies a refinement process, getting down to the basics of what truly matters. The emotions of grief and courage are central to the autumn season. Times of grief and loss are often an opportunity for resolving issues and learning life lessons, letting you know what you value in life. Just as nature at this time of year is letting go of what it no longer needs, you are encouraged to do the same. The element of Metal requires courage to face the question of what in your current life circumstances gives you value—and what you need to let go of.

When balanced in Metal, you are authentic, courageous, self-disciplined, and navigate your life with integrity. When out of balance, not feeling your inner strength, you find yourself creating excessive rules and exhibiting a controlling nature.

There was a time when my life was organized down to every tiny detail, full of "dos and don'ts," as I strived to make everything perfect. This tendency had me labeling everything as right or wrong, good or bad, while emotionally detaching from others as a protective measure—a common consequence for an imbalanced Metal.

A Metal imbalance can leave you brittle. If you continue restricting life and micromanaging, this inflexibility would make you start questioning your authenticity and leave you vulnerable to be molded by others. This is the exact opposite of what the Metal essence can provide. This imbalance will be revealed through coldness (hands/feet), lower back stiffness, and decreased circulation leading to respiratory issues, such as shortness of breath or asthma, skin eruptions, and internal inflammatory responses (sinusitis/laryngitis) that cannot heal because of an inability to let go of what cannot be controlled. You will have lost your inner courage.

Physical Organs. The Metal phase is governed by the lungs and the large intestines. Your inner state is reflected in your breath and bowels. Bringing awareness to your breath can enhance your ability to center and relax. Breath is life, the connection between all bodily functions, healing and merging mind and body. As you take in a breath, you can only hold it for so long before you need to exhale, a natural and inevitable form of letting go.

The large intestines also contribute to the process of letting go. Being the organ of elimination, the intestines physically remove bodily wastes, but energetically they signify letting go of personal principles and hardwired and conditioned beliefs that no longer serve you.

Climate. Autumn brings in strong, dry winds, pushing energy in and downward. You can easily feel the dry wind on your skin as it enters in and influences the lungs. This time of year focuses on a dietary pattern to keep the lungs moist and clear, promote the circulation of qi/blood, and support digestive health.

Food Recommendations. At this time, nature is providing an abundance of root vegetables with inward and downward energetic properties, making it a time for yams, turnips, parsnips, burdock, rutabaga, beets, celeriac, daikon, and squash. Counteracting the dryness through moistening foods will assist in clearing respiratory passages and reestablishing qi circulation and movement through digestive processes. Moistening foods include barley, millet, soybeans, mushrooms, almonds, walnuts, pumpkin, seaweeds, and navy and lima beans.

To stay on a strengthening dietary pattern for protected lungs, digestive health, and qi or blood circulation, continue a strategy of eating cooked foods. Shift to techniques of simmering, baking, pressure-cooking, and roasting. Think thick stews and soups and longer cooking times, making it easier to digest and be nurtured through a watery medium. Baked fruits, such as warm apples with cardamom and poached pears with star anise and cinnamon, are good choices for this season.

Autumn is a time to add additional protein to your diet; however, excessive animal-based products produce phlegm and exacerbate an uptight personality—a highlighted challenge of this season.

Flavor. Pungent is the flavor of the Metal phase, dispersing energy up and out, encouraging the movement of qi/blood, clearing the sinuses, and stimulating the lungs. Pungent foods include garlic, onion, fennel, ginger, scallions, nutmeg, dill, and chives. Add these to your stews and soups for flavor enhancement as well as health-stimulating effect.

General Recommendations. Autumn is the time to slow down, take naps, meditate, and retire early. Take a moment to bring awareness to *you*. Are you feeling an unwavering inner courage? Or is there an imbalance in mind, body, or soul that needs more nourishment to resolve?

Start preparing for the upcoming months of introspection and turning within. The winter months are right around the corner.

Autumn Eating Strategies

- Emphasize plant-based diet with small amounts of animal foods.
- Eat an abundance of root vegetables.
- Keep the pungent flavor dominant.
- Keep foods of a warming nature in meals.
- Incorporate moistening foods to combat the season's dryness.
- Remain hydrated while adding fiber-rich foods to aid elimination.
- Choose cooked rather than raw preparations.
- Cooking preparations include poaching, simmering, pressure-cooking, and roasting.
- Add additional protein into the diet, such as legumes, fish, and some land animal.
- Slow down and begin using food preparation as a meditation time.

The Water Element: Winter

The Water element of winter brings us full cycle to wholeness. In this phase, everything begins and ends and then begins again to mark a rebirth and creation of another Wood phase, the spring. It is in Water, the wintertime, that the creative ideas and plans of the spring originate.

WATER ELEMENT

Season: Winter
Essence: Wholeness
Organs: Kidneys/Bladder
Climate: Cold
Flavor: Salty

Essence and Personal Traits. Winter is a time when everything ends but also begins anew, symbolizing the Universe's constant recycling and wholeness. An example is seen in how a day unfolds. The sun rises in the Wood phase, goes through the day in Fire, transitions out of the day in Earth, starts to settle down into the evening in Metal, and turns in for sleep in the Water phase. All phases operate in a larger movement and are continuously connected.

Water is the essential medium of the body, taking on the form of its container and showing its adaptability and versatility. When Water is balanced, you are introspective, somewhat of a philosopher, a person of curiosity, seeking a perspective about life beyond the mundane world. With a thriving imagination, you can get lost in your thoughts of appreciating winter's gifts of stillness and solitude. When out of balance, the emotion of fear takes over. You may choose to hibernate during this time for reasons of anxiety and phobias. The physical body reflects this state of mind with stiff joints, arthritic conditions, artery hardening, and fluid retention.

Physical Organs. The Water element is governed by the kidneys and bladder. In TCM, the kidneys are referred to as the body's pilot light, storing jing, our human essence that is a determining factor of longevity. Your kidneys are responsible for filtering blood and for the production and regulation of hormones to control blood pressure, produce red blood cells, and maintain the strength and integrity of the bones. The bladder eliminates excess fluid, with dysfunction in the bladder being linked to a person's coping and adaptability challenges.

Climate. The winter season is a time to rest and retreat. With the climate of cold, you will naturally slow down, seek warmth, and hibernate. Nature is still, and there's a sensation of calm in the air, creating the perfect setting for reflection and regeneration. This is the time to listen more deeply within and learn about yourself. You can't always be on the go; your energy and resources need time to replenish.

Food Recommendations. A dietary pattern to remain in harmony with Water is one that generates heat, strengthens the digestive system, and nourishes the heart. Your intuitive sense will already draw you toward warming foods. Winter brings out the best in recipes for congees, soups, and stews. Introducing warming foods in a watery medium and cooked for an extended time maintains digestive health and strengthens the kidneys, keeping blood and qi flowing.

Pressure-cooking, broiling, braising, and roasting are also recommended. Regardless of preparation technique, foods have their own innate thermal nature. This is a post-digestive temperature that affects the body's thermostat. Some foods are physiologically cool and lower body temperature, while others are warming, generating heat and elevating body temperature. Warming foods include black beans, tempeh, kale, squash, sweet potato, carrots, coconut, walnut, fennel, leeks, and onions. Warming herbs and spices include cinnamon, cardamom, garlic, ginger, cumin, rosemary, and basil.

Protein consumption remains high in winter, as with the autumn season. Because of their connection to Water element, fish and seaweeds can be added for additional protein, in keeping with the essence of going with the flow and adaptability to change. Adding some animal in the form of grass-fed, pasture-raised beef can be helpful to those struggling with the stillness in this phase.

Flavor. The salty flavor resonates with the winter season and penetrates the kidneys and bladder, regulating water metabolism and alleviating dryness. Incorporate the salty flavor through cooking with a quality sea salt and foods, such as seaweed, barley, millet, and miso.

Salt brings energy down and inward and has centering qualities that are beneficial in times possibly dominated by the emotion of fear. Salt is also moistening, enhances digestion, and can provide a sense of calmness.

General Recommendations. During the wintertime, engage in light exercise, sleep a little more, and allow yourself to daydream with the ultimate goal of keeping life simple. You are looking into a time of rebirth coming up in spring, and you want to be prepared for the full cycle of nature beginning yet again.

Eating Strategies for Winter

- Emphasize a plant-based dietary pattern with the addition of animal foods.
- Eat foods with a warming thermal nature.
- Add warming spices and herbs to aid in digestion.
- Bring in the salty flavor for its winter balancing qualities.
- Incorporate moistening foods to alleviate winter's dryness.
- Incorporate fish and seaweeds.
- Add more protein—the highest consumption of the year.
- Make congees, soups, and stews part of your daily regimen.
- Cooking preparation includes pressure cooking, braising, roasting, and broiling.
- Avoid phlegm-producing foods: dairy, juices, sugar, and processed starches.

****

Congratulations—you have completed stage 2 of your transformational journey through food! As you move on to stage 3, know that your entire journey is based on self-awareness, which is the willingness to look within. The mere act of self-observation makes everyday decisions easier as you align with your best interests at the time.

Daily Self-Assessment Tool

As you move between stage 2 and stage 3, continue to use your self-assessment tool to help align your food choices with nature and the seasons. By the time you finish stage 3, you will have a complete tool to use in making sure that you are getting the full hidden messages in food.

Use the questions below as a scan to do daily, preferably in the morning as you are getting ready for your day.

The first ten questions below are from the Stage 1 Self-Assessment Tool, repeated here so you can see the added layer of elements from stage 2. What new nutritional strategies will you employ to align yourself with nature and find balance within?

Stage 2 Self-Assessment Tool

1. Overall, how are you feeling (present, relaxed, calm, distracted, anxious, annoyed, or other)?
2. How are your energy levels (ready to go, light and alert, tired, heaviness in body, or other)?
3. Are you feeling internally hot or cold? How do your hands and feet feel?
4. Are you hydrated?
5. How are your bowel movements (diarrhea, constipated, daily frequency, or other)?
6. Do you feel dry (skin, throat, digestive system), or do you feel damp (bloated, swelling, congested)?
7. Was your diet in the past day, more alkaline or acidic?
8. Have your recent meal choices been more whole foods or more processed?
9. Are you eating a lot of animal? Any particular one?
10. What environment are you eating your meals in (peaceful, disruptive, with company, alone, or other)?
11. What season is it? What element is dominant? How about physical organs?
12. What is the weather outside like (hot, cold, rainy, dry, or other)?

13. What is your internal weather (overheated, cold, congested, dry, or other)?
14. How are you incorporating the flavor of the season into your meals?
15. What cooking techniques would be the most serving of your health goals today?

STAGE 3

Let Food Align You with Your Source

Welcome to stage 3 of transforming your relationship with food for a more authentic life.

In stage 1, "Food beyond the Calorie," you explored the full potential of food and gained a new understanding of food's physical and energetic intelligence. Stage 2, "Eating in Sync with the Seasons," took you to another layer of food's potential by showing you how to connect your food choices and practices with the rhythms of nature. In stage 3, you incorporate all you've learned in the first two stages to further expand your awareness into the spiritual dimension, adding the powerful relationship food can have with the Universe, your Higher Self, Source, the Divine, God, or whatever you choose to call it.

CHAPTER 5

CHAKRA NUTRITION

Eating food is a daily necessity that invites continuous awareness, making it the perfect guide for healing and self-exploration. In stage 3, you move closer to your authentic self through chakra nutrition. I use the term *chakra nutrition* for exploring nutrition through what in Eastern teachings is known as the chakra system.

What Is a Chakra?

Chakras are vortexes of energy that run from the base of the spine to the crown of the head, parallel to the spinal cord. There are seven main chakras in the human chakra system, each one named for its position on the ascending chakra ladder: the root chakra, the sacral chakra, the solar plexus chakra, the heart chakra, the throat chakra, the third eye chakra, and the crown chakra.

Chakras act as regulators of the life-force energy, or qi, that we receive from the Universe, animating us in our physical bodies. Each of these seven energy centers vibrates at a particular frequency and wavelength linked to specific biological processes. Chakras are the place where our minds and bodies, the energetic and physical aspects of life, unite.

Each chakra has a focus based on the level of consciousness that it represents, with the life force linking to the universal source where it originated. Each chakra can be understood for its essential nature, the life lessons it teaches, and corresponding physiological processes. Continuous unimpeded flow of qi through the chakras and throughout the body's meridian or energy pathways determines overall well-being.

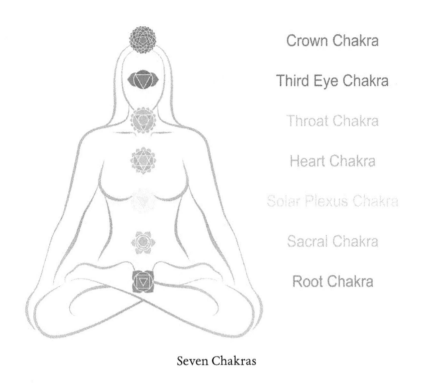

Crown Chakra

Third Eye Chakra

Throat Chakra

Heart Chakra

Solar Plexus Chakra

Sacral Chakra

Root Chakra

Seven Chakras

Each chakra's vibrational frequency manifests as a color and corresponds to specific food flavors and colors.

Chakra	Color	Food Examples
root	red	tomato, raspberries, beets, apples
sacral	orange	apricots, carrots, peaches, sweet potato
solar plexus	yellow	lemons, corn, summer squash, banana
heart	green	kale, avocado, kiwi, broccoli
throat	blue	blueberries, juniper berries
third eye	indigo	eggplant, fig, pluot, blackberries
crown	white	onions, garlic, jicama, fennel

Chakra Anatomy 101

An understanding of how the chakra system unites both energetic and physical aspects of your being will help you to see how your food choices interact with each one.

The universal energy, or qi, enters your body through the crown of your head. It travels down along energy currents that correspond to the nerve ganglia. There are major energy currents and a series of channels for energy circulation. The major energy flow runs down the center of the spine and is called the *Sushumna*.

The Sushumna corresponds to the central nervous system (CNS) as defined in Western science. The CNS consists of two major organs: the brain and spinal cord. Your brain processes and interprets sensory information to coordinate your body's functions. The spinal cord acts like a conduit for the exchange of signals that go back and forth between your brain and the rest of your body.

There are two additional energy currents running alongside the Sushumna called *Ida* and *Pingala*. The Ida rules the left side of your body, representing the receptive principle of the universal energy, or yin, and corresponds to the parasympathetic nervous system (PNS). The Pingala rules the right side of your body, representing the active principle of the universal energy, or yang, and corresponds to the sympathetic nervous system (SNS). The PNS conserves energy and promotes recovery and rest, while the SNS is your fight-or-flight response when under stress.

Yin and yang, the PNS and SNS, are part of the greater autonomic nervous system (ANS) that coordinates your body's involuntary actions, such as heart rate, digestion, respiratory rate, perspiration, and urinary functions. The Ida and Pingala crisscross over the Sushumna to meet at specific points along the spinal column, bringing yin and yang together and marking locations of each of the seven chakras.

Everything in nature comes down to finding and maintaining balance. In balance, you experience a free flow of energy that allows you to receive and express within that level of consciousness while remaining grounded yet expansive in your thoughts and actions.

In chakra anatomy, this is reflected by distinct currents of energy flow connecting you to both physical and spiritual realms. The current of manifestation flows downward to connect you to the physical world where your thoughts take form, and the current of freedom flows upward toward a more abstract and cosmic perspective. When in balance, your energy is flowing freely, and you are experiencing your authentic self.

You can think of the chakra system as a ladder to climb, the steps leading you from a focus on physical existence to one that is more spiritual. Grounded in the Earth, the system provides the energetic stability for you to function in the physical world. As you travel up the chakras, your energetic being elevates in vibration and plays a larger part in your life. Your perspectives change. You gain a more cosmic outlook on life. This creates an opportunity to experience life at a depth past the ordinary.

When physiological symptoms or illness arises, it can be viewed as an expression of universal, spiritual energy on the physical plane. There is a deeper layer to physical experiences that can be tracked back through the corresponding chakra to the root of the manifestation. Struggles with weight loss, unrelenting acid reflux, debilitating migraines, and chronic lower back pain are all invitations to explore current life circumstances asking for your attention. For example, chronic lower back pain is correlated with the sacral chakra, which points to underlying lessons about flowing with life's changes. Behind the lower back pain there may be some form of resistance manifesting as stagnation and the need to be in control.

The chakras connect you to your true nature—body, mind, and soul. When you look at the human being as mere flesh and organs, your attention gets placed on only one aspect of who you are. In the chakra system, your spiritual lessons are built into your biological design with the divine intelligence running through you, providing the energy that animates you, giving the gift of life and allowing for your human experience. Healing from an illness or proactively exploring preventive measures for your health requires an investigation into all aspects of who you are. Becoming mindful of both your energetic and physical beings will bring you into a state of wholeness.

Chakra Imbalance

We all have our ways of dealing with life's challenges. Some run for the hills, others simply ignore the elephant in the room, and still others go full force at the situation with varying degrees of obsession. But whatever your coping strategies are, they become conditioned patterns of behavior that impact energy flow to your chakras, blocking a chakra at times or throwing it off balance. Depending on what emotional state you are in, you can weaken your ability to express or receive the life lesson that is presenting itself through a particular chakra. Or worse, the result of an imbalanced chakra can show up as a physical illness, a chronic emotional struggle, or stagnant and often debilitating belief systems.

There are two emotional states you can be in to profoundly affect the balance of your chakras. These are love and fear. Love is a space of growth, while fear is a state of protection. You are creating your life and living in love and growth, or you are surviving your life and living in fear and protection.

When you live in a space of love, you are open to the world. Life is viewed as filled with opportunities, not obstacles. You are grounded yet flexible in nature. You are able to step out of your box of thinking, be more spontaneous, and not always need to be in control. In this state of love, you are able to have an exchange with the Universe, and when you stop attempting to micromanage your experiences, that's when life happens.

If you live in a state of fear, you are in a protective mode. This happens in acute circumstances, a natural part of our defenses; however, when you stay in this state for long periods of time, it restricts your growth, halting self-healing processes by blocking the universal energy from flowing freely through the chakras.

Your body is a self-healing entity in which every single cell constantly regenerates itself. This means that within seven to ten years, you are physically an entirely new person. Think about that for a moment. You are designed to continuously grow, regenerate, and evolve, and when you embrace your true nature, you have found the key to a life of good health and longevity—the life you were meant to live.

What State Are You In—Love or Fear?

- Are your everyday emotions ones of gratitude or sadness?
- Do you feel grounded in your current life circumstances, or is life unreliable?
- Do you see new experiences as opportunities or obstacles?
- Are you comfortable with spontaneous events, or do you crave routine?
- Are you flexible, or do you want control?

The Chakras and Your Food Choices

When you understand chakras as the link between universal consciousness and physical manifestation, the food you put in your body becomes nourishment for your body, mind, and soul. For example, at the level of the solar plexus chakra, there is an interdependent relationship between carbohydrate foods, digestion, and self-esteem. All three are operating at the same level of consciousness that is focused at the solar plexus chakra.

In addition, your behaviors surrounding your food choices are linked to a particular chakra's underlying universal meaning. From cravings for sweets, an aversion to fish, or why you like to eat until you feel full to struggles with balancing hormones—all of these are reflections of who you are and the current circumstances of your life, along with the universal life lesson that is asking for your attention.

With each conscious connection you make, you reveal another dimension of who you are. With every step you take toward understanding yourself, you bring the healing process into action. Food is the initiator of this process, assisting in shifting the energy flow to the chakras and impacting the current health status of your mind-body. As physical symptoms settle, and your body begins to restore itself, you have an opportunity to reflect on the underlying consciousness, those thought patterns at the origin of the physical manifestations you are experiencing.

The choice is before you: Do you want to remove physical ailments on the surface level with a high probability of their return, going about your life as you know it? Or do you want to dig a little deeper to get to the hidden messages, to grasp how your life is asking for your attention, and perhaps make changes that will bring you closer to remembering your wholeness? Consider that the deeper solution brings with it an added bonus of more permanent results and lasting change.

What's to Come ...

In stage 3, you will be introduced to each of the seven chakras' overall characteristics, including their essences and personal life lessons, as well their connections to physical organs and specific food traits. You will also read about strategies, complementary exercises, and self-reflection questions to help you address your own challenges. All of this provides support to begin climbing the chakra ladder to discover your wider connection to the Universe and your authentic self.

And it all begins with getting grounded. Let me introduce you first to your root chakra.

CHAPTER 6

ROOT CHAKRA: GETTING GROUNDED

ROOT CHAKRA

Essence: Security and Belonging
Life Lesson: Becoming Grounded
Physical: Immunity/Digestion/Bone
Food: Protein
Flavor: Sweet
Color: Red

Located at the base of the spine, the root chakra is the foundation for all the other chakras, providing a space of stability and reliability, the essential aspects for a healthy and expansive life.

Essential Nature: Security and Belonging

The anchor of any path of healing and personal evolution is becoming grounded in the root chakra. Feeling grounded provides security, a sense of belonging, and a connection to the physical world—all parts of the essential nature of the root chakra.

The root chakra energy can be felt through your physical structure and its contact with Mother Earth. You also developed this grounding through your initial family relationships and environment. Your upbringing taught you beliefs, attitudes, and behaviors that supported the family's safety in the physical world.

When standing in the consciousness of the root chakra, you are submerged in the physical world with self-preservation as your first priority. It is all about survival needs, taking care of your everyday living needs, which are safety, food, and shelter.

In this chakra, you are your most instinctual or primitive self. You rely solely on the five senses for information about the world and find yourself seeking connection with others in the form of blood family, cultural traditions, and even religious sects. I feel the root chakra's grounding energy when cheering for the women's national soccer team playing for the World Cup.

At this chakra, you develop your beliefs about "home," the place you return to in order to find your center in the midst of life's challenges and adventures. Although initially influenced by childhood experiences, home is not a physical place but a deep space within you at your core, reflective of your connection to the Universe.

What does it mean to be grounded? Grounding is established through the connection your physical body feels with Mother Earth. It's not a coincidence that we often seek nature to find peace, calmness, or a way to destress from life's challenges. You may head to the beach and listen to the waves, take to the park for a hike, or simply put your bare feet in the grass. The Earth's resonance and frequency removes excess electrical activity from your bio-field, allowing for a space of tranquility. Being in nature allows you to feel connected to something bigger than yourself. As you saw in stage 2, aligning with the seasons gives you a new sense of belonging. Each of us is a miniature universe, reflecting the greater Universe outside of us.

Think of your physical body as your home base. Knowing yourself to be an energetic being as well as a physical one, see your body as a vehicle of your spirit, or soul. Whether you believe you are a spiritual being having a human experience or the reverse, if will benefit you to be able to work within both worlds.

When operating purely from the five senses with the focus on everyday, immediate needs, choices are about safety, boundaries, and loyalty. These topics continually emerge to demonstrate separation and debate within and among different groups of people. Yet the underlying essence of the root chakra is "All is one." Oneness can be a challenging concept to embrace with so much ongoing prejudice, discrimination, and segregation occurring in our world. As a human population, we still struggle with a sense of safety and grounding, keeping us in our conditioned beliefs and acting out of fear. This is reflected in the growing obesity epidemic, escalation of immune-based diseases, and rise in social/ cultural injustices.

As author Mike Dooley points out in *Leveraging the Universe*, "We need to behave physically but with a spiritual awareness." This means bringing awareness to your physical body and its needs while remaining connected to the Universe. As a society, we strongly emphasize intellect, achievement, and material growth, and certainly there is nothing wrong with sharpening our intellect, completing a project, or creating material abundance. It is when those activities are done at the expense of our connection to the physical body and the Universe that problems arise.

Life Lessons: Becoming Grounded

When your instinctual survival energy of the root chakra is balanced, you have a strong sense of who you are with well-defined boundaries and a sense of connection to all that is. Having this sense of security and connection to yourself and the physical world creates an opportunity to begin exploring life outside your current circumstances. You are more prone to step outside the box, entertain curiosity, and step toward an unfamiliar adventure if you feel like you have an anchor or home of support behind you.

It's natural to want your survival needs addressed before adding more to your life. Yet sometimes these survival needs are not met. You may find yourself jumping out into life without an anchor, chasing big dreams yet incapable of seeing them manifest. Or you may respond like many do, keeping a tight grip on wherever you found a sense of belonging, seeking routine with an aversion to unplanned or spontaneous events. This gives a false sense of security and control, leading to stagnation in your individual evolution.

The first step in recognizing your level of grounding is to bring your awareness to your physical body. For some time, I lived in my intellect, completely detached from my body to the point that expressing my physical discomfort was vague and for the most part incomprehensible.

I know I wasn't alone in this scenario; most people I've consulted with have had survival and safety struggles. After all, it's a universal life lesson to learn how to feel at home in your own physical body.

Becoming grounded gives a sense of safety from which to reach beyond other people's perspectives and go toward your own personal aspirations and passions. Choosing to go in the direction of your dreams regardless of the opinions of others is a tall feat. The first step in making this a possibility is getting out of your head and into your body. The root chakra is where you will find your center and ground.

Addressing the Food Tribe

Community and the sense of belonging are essential to the health of the root chakra. But with this yearning for community and acceptance comes the root chakra's greatest challenge, the willingness and inner courage to step away from traditional, family, or group perspectives about food and health in order to explore what best serves you as an individual at this particular time in your life.

This is not an easy undertaking, especially with the growing number of "food tribes" surfacing through the media. The conversation quite often goes to the question of, What tribe are you in? Are you Paleo? Raw? Vegan? Flexitarian? There's a natural hunger to connect with others yet giving yourself a fixed identity can limit your potential.

When you are grounded, you are willing to explore and make new choices surrounding food and life, choices that may not reflect those of the current company you keep, whether friends, family, or traditional culture. The reality is when you change your relationship with food, there will be a ripple effect into other aspects of your life. Every part of you is touched by every change, no matter how minor it may seem at the time. No wonder diets so often fail! You get to the point that requires real action, and instead you retreat to old behaviors. Diets do not peel back the layers of who you are, asking you to address your relationship with food, others, and the world.

Moving away from group perspectives in search of your authentic self is the beginning of your journey to heal and evolve. Keep the traditions that serve you and have the courage to make decisions that you know reflect your current interests and needs. If you stay in your tribe's perspective, you will evolve only at the rate of that group. It is one thing to develop community for connection, but it's another thing to rely on it for grounding. As much as people may think they know you, you are the only one who truly knows what you think, need, feel, and wish for.

Remember—as you step out from a tribe you've ascribed to, you are creating the space for others to follow. Others may get upset with you, making comments like "Since when do you eat like that?" because you are shifting your identity and therefore your relationships with them. The truth is new choices may not always be met with support and can even cause disruption in the family order. Don't be surprised if others try to sabotage your new way of living—it's only human nature to react to change with fear. But I can only say to that—*keep rocking the boat!*

Physiology of the Root Chakra

This root chakra is linked to your physical structure and immune defenses, all elements pointing to survival and instinct. To get balanced at this level, begin by observing your current state of physical health. Are you experiencing any physical ailments that are reflective of not being able to defend or protect yourself as you interact with your environment? This can develop as overall fatigue, autoimmune illness, inflammatory issues, excessive weight gain, digestive dysfunction, circulatory issues such as hypertension or varicose veins, and bone/muscle issues of the lower extremities.

Beyond the physical response is your emotional and mental response to survival needs. If those needs are not being met, you might develop an inflexible nature, fixed in routine and habit with an underlying anxiety and even depression. You may even become clingy or meddlesome in other people's affairs, attempting to secure a sense of belonging in the world. Yearning to belong can cause you to sacrifice your true self, stifling your potential and putting you on a socially accepted path that you are not aligned with.

When you find your ground, you give yourself permission to express yourself to the world, regardless of the judgment, criticism, or approval of others. This grounding will come from within, and when it does, your outer world will change dramatically with every choice you make and move you closer toward your truth.

Let's look at issues related to root chakra physiology: immunity, digestion, and bone health.

Immunity and Digestion. A strong immunity allows us to interact with the external world. The immune system not only is a protective mechanism against foreign pathogens but can also be seen as a communicative sensory organ that observes, interprets, and responds to external stimuli while monitoring cell to cell interaction.

Maintaining a strong immunity starts with the health of your digestive system. The digestive tract is home to 70 percent of the immune system since it is one of the initial interfaces with the external world, the lungs being the second. The digestive tract is thirty feet long with a lining that is only one quarter the thickness of a sheet of paper. Your body naturally repairs and regenerates this lining every three to four days with the intention of maintaining its integrity and preventing any damage. Damage to the intestinal lining disrupts the digestive system's ability to filter what passes through into the blood or lymph of the body.

Digestion is more than simply a way to break down food, feed your grumbling stomach, and provide energy. Your ability to digest food will affect your immune status, ability to assimilate nutrients, capacity for detoxification, and even your state of mind. The first approach to immunity is to support the two main organs of the digestive system, the stomach and spleen, the organs corresponding to the Earth element. The most beneficial foods for strengthening immunity are whole foods with antioxidant, anti-inflammatory, and antiviral properties. These properties can be found in deeply colored foods, such as blackberries, plums, beets and cherries. A category of plant foods called cruciferous vegetables— brussels sprouts, watercress, arugula, broccoli, and cauliflower—have strong immune-enhancing and detoxifying properties. Foods with pungent flavors contain health-promoting compounds, adding scallions, onions, garlic, leeks, and ginger to the list. The entire mushroom family including portabella, shiitake, and cremini embodies the grounding essence and is full of immune-impacting phytonutrients.

If you are experiencing food sensitivities and allergies, it may indicate a compromised immune response and an inflamed internal environment with deeper messages of an imbalanced root chakra. Remember the root is about survival and safety in the physical world. If you continuously feel off-center, lack connection, or are experiencing instability, the body responds to that state of being. A low-grade stress, causing a low-grade, continuous release of adrenal hormones, will disrupt the entire network of the immune, endocrine, and nervous system. You end up living in a fight or flight state, with your immunity suffering. This is why people get colds when they are run down.

Food and the Root Chakra

Food is part of survival, connecting you to Mother Earth and keeping you in touch with your physical body. What better way to get grounded than through the food you choose to eat?

Using a blend of Eastern teachings and modern science, we will explore how particular foods—protein sources, root vegetables, and the sweet flavor—impact energy flow to the root chakra, initiating and enhancing your experience of being grounded.

Protein. We ground through our physical bodies and our connection to Mother Earth, and one of the main nutrients we need in order to do this is protein.

Protein is part of muscles and bones and therefore forms the main support of the physical body through what's called a *collagen matrix*. Collagen is what determines bone flexibility. Protein has many other roles within the body and is touted as the superior nutrient to consume. With each diet that hits the bookshelves, there is a growing emphasis on consuming greater amounts of protein. I see this protein campaign as reflecting the increasing lack of grounding in our society, resulting in epidemic rates of obesity, increase of autoimmune illness, and the rising fear of community and national security.

Without going into a debate over high or low protein consumption, let's explore some possible protein sources and leave the ratio of daily protein consumption up to the individual. You will soon see how the amount of protein you choose to put into your diet is directly related to the health of your root chakra.

Animal sources of protein. In our society, protein has become synonymous with animal foods. But while animal foods contain a high percentage of protein, there are also other factors to consider when choosing protein sources for your diet. Most important is the vibrational essence of the animal.

Animals represent an instinctual, survival-based essence. They are grounded and live in the present moment. When you consume animal flesh, you take in the innate essence of their species as well as the energetic vibration of the animal's life.

Each animal has a vibrational energy that reflects the innate nature of that species. For example, pigs are one of the most sociable animals, and if raised in their natural habitat, spend the days interacting with one another to gather twigs, branches, and leaves used to sleep together. Their vibrational frequency is one of loyalty and community. Chickens are also highly sociable and, when in their natural living environment, have a hierarchy or pecking order. They instinctually know their rank in a flock of almost one hundred chickens. Their vibrational frequency is one of independence and pride. These vibrational energies interact with ours when we eat them.

Consider the impact on vibrational energy if these animals were not living in their natural habitats but instead in factory farms and isolated in cages, having their biological urges violated and arriving at slaughterhouses suffering from countless diseases. Do you think this has any impact on your vibrational energy? You bet it does. I'm not saying this to deter you from consuming animal-based products, but rather to create a heightened awareness of respect and gratitude for animals that have had their lives sacrificed. Perhaps with a change in attitude, we'd see the animals we eat living in a more natural environment, pasture raised with space to roam, fed their appropriate diet, and interacting as designed with their fellow peeps.

With this in mind, ask yourself the following: Which animals do I gravitate toward? Which are my favorites? Which do I not like to eat at all? Look at the vibrational essences of the animals below. What essence are you attracting into your life by eating the animals you choose to eat? Now that's a worthy contemplation to have with yourself.

Essence of Animals

Animal	Energetic Essence
bison	abundance, sign of prosperity
chicken	sociable, territorial, pride, egoic, inner courage
cow	nurturing, patient, calming, social connection
deer	grace, a mix of determination and gentleness, intuition
duck	resourcefulness, sense of knowing, self-confidence
goat	independence, curiosity, honor oneself, look within
pig	honesty, loyalty, good luck
rabbit	rebirth, longevity, grounding, earthly
sheep	innocence, vulnerability, self-acceptance
squirrel	balance, playful, preparation, resourceful
turkey	renewal, generosity, gratitude

There are other considerations when choosing animal-based protein sources. The more animal you consume, the slower your vibrational energy becomes, and the more instinctual you become. Daily consumption of animal-based foods can make you aggressive, stubborn, and fixed in routine. They literally make you more animalistic. There's no room for expansion and change in these circumstances.

Additionally, animal-based products alter biochemistry differently than plant-based foods do. Animal-based foods produce arachidonic acid, which produces prostaglandins, hormone-like compounds that not only cause a systemic inflammatory response within the body but also stimulate neurotransmitters such as glutamate that lead to nerve cell death. This nerve cell death has detrimental effects on learning and memory, taking you away from the gifts of neuroplasticity and improved brain function and closer to more primitive physiology.

Keeping all this in mind and letting go of the belief that protein has to equate with meat, consider other sources to fulfill your need for this essential nutrient and provide additional root chakra nourishment. Plant-based protein is more bioavailable by design and, through the production of prostaglandins that yield an anti-inflammatory effect and an alkaline ash supportive of the body's self-healing and regeneration processes, may be a better choice. Protein-rich plant sources include tempeh, lentils, adzuki beans, almonds, and collard greens. In plants, we find not only protein but fiber, phytonutrients, vitamins, and minerals that all work together to elicit a grounding effect, support bone integrity, and strengthen immunity.

As you shift to placing more emphasis on plant-based foods, you might become more aware of how inflexible or fixed in thought and action you have been in your life. The invitation to acknowledge and even address that hidden message in food becomes possible as you allow yourself to experience more freedom and spontaneity in your self-expression.

Root Vegetables and Bone Health. When we are thinking grounding and survival, let's remember our connection to Mother Earth. Walking the boardwalk on a sunny afternoon, hearing the waves crash, or sinking your knees into the soil to prune and care for your garden—all these activities remind us of our connection. The Earth element rules the root chakra, another reminder of the qualities of stability and strength. Take a look at a tree; it's firm yet flexible, with its roots deep into the Earth.

Root vegetables grow deep into the Earth and have the exact grounding vibration we seek for strengthening our connection to Mother Earth. Consider adding beets, carrots, daikon, gingerroot, onions, parsnips, yams, and radishes to your dietary pattern. Along with their grounding vibration, you will find these foods rich in fiber, providing a sense of fullness while regulating your blood sugar levels and digestive health.

Plant-based foods can also deliver essential minerals that are crucial to bone health and thus structural integrity. The talk of osteoporosis and bone health can be a lengthy discussion full of debate, especially on the topic of calcium needs. Whatever your beliefs on the topic, keep in mind that the integrity of our bones is a complex process within the body that is controlled by hormones and influenced by the ratios of minerals (not the amount of just one, calcium). Bone strength and integrity is also affected by additional dietary and lifestyle choices, such as sugar, caffeine, physical movement, and our struggles with finding our center. Foods that support bone integrity include brussels sprouts, mustard greens, bok choy, figs, cauliflower, and kale. Load up on the bitter leafy greens and cruciferous vegetables, and you won't go wrong.

Flavor of Sweet. Ever have a craving for something with a sweet flavor? I think just hearing the word *sweet* makes us smile and think of many of our favorite comfort foods. The sweet flavor is connected to the root chakra and TCM's Earth element.

Foods with a sweet flavor go beyond those that are made of concentrated, processed sugars. Meat, dairy, juices, wheat, and nuts are also on the top of the sweet-flavor list. Vegetables are there too, just with a different digestible effect. The concern becomes how much of the sweet flavor is too much? If we consume too much sweet food, we experience what is called dampness in TCM, a topic discussed in more detail in stage 2. Dampness impairs digestion and over time leads to mucous, congestion, water retention, development of candida or fungi, and weight gain. A state of sluggishness and stagnancy becomes established throughout the mind-body. Over time, the presence of dampness creates diseases of inflammation. This is yet another reason to assess the amount of meat and even dairy in your daily food choices.

Red and Green Foods. As mentioned previously, your chakras vibrate at specific frequencies, with the root chakra having the slowest frequency, drawing you into the Earth in order to become grounded. Colors are the physical manifestations of these frequencies, with the color red resonating with the root chakra. Foods that are red, as well as red's complimentary color of green, interact with your vibration, causing an energy exchange and drawing more flow to the root chakra. Try bringing awareness to the colors you are drawn to or have an aversion to. This observation can assist you to understand what areas in your life are currently seeking your attention.

Be conscious of adding red- and green-colored foods to your diet, especially in times of grounding and reestablishing your center. It is not a coincidence that many health advocates suggest eating a rainbow diet full of a variety of colored foods. Many of those health-supportive compounds, or phytonutrients, are found within the colors of the food, boosting immunity, influencing gene expression, and also forming an energetic connection to a specific chakra and its deeper level of universal consciousness.

Strategies for Balance

Through your relationship with food, you can begin to understand your body's daily needs of nourishment while being connected to Mother Earth and all other beings. When you feel rooted, you are strong and balanced in all your relationships. Grounding will allow you to remain centered and empowered regardless of life's circumstances. This is the beginning of getting into the driver's seat and co-creating your life.

A good practice to nourish the root chakra involves going outdoors to enjoy your meals. Any opportunity to have a picnic, eat at the beach, or even an outdoor café will give you a sense of connection to nature. Flip off those shoes, and put your feet in the grass or sand. Don't worry about being "proper"—finding your grounding is not about conforming.

Another strategy is to create a community to share and exchange recipes. Take it one step further and share your culinary creations with friends or neighbors. There is no need to freeze your extra food—giving food to others is an act that nurtures your root chakra.

There are so many ways to get grounded, spending time in nature being the easiest and most effective. Do any outdoor activity you love. Hit the hiking trails, go for a walk on the beach, or simply sit on a blanket in the park with your feet in the grass. Ideally be barefoot. Sitting or standing, get yourself out into nature. My favorite way to do this is to do the yoga tree pose out on the grass. Do it daily, even if it is only for a few minutes.

Take the time and demonstrate that you are worth this journey. And if you really want to find your footing, go hop on a NYC subway and keep your balance on that train ride without holding on to the center pole. You'll feel that connection right through your soles, and it's guaranteed to make you smile.

Root Chakra Strategies for Balance

- Emphasize plant-based protein.
- Eat sweet flavor in form of root vegetables, grains, and legumes.
- Add pungent flavors to remove stagnancy.
- Eat red- and green-colored foods.
- Incorporate immune-boosting foods: cruciferous vegetables, bitter greens and mushrooms.
- Eat meals cooked, not raw/cold nature.
- Eat outdoors whenever possible.
- Share recipes and food with others.
- Eat only until 70 percent full.

Self-Reflection Questions

To increase your awareness of the root chakra, take a moment to contemplate the following questions. Be honest with yourself. Sometimes shadow behaviors are difficult to embrace. View them as teachers and messengers, meaning look at yourself with compassion.

The fact that you are seeking a higher level of awareness already says so much about your efforts to heal and evolve. Keep in mind that your nutrition needs will continue to evolve as you do, so you may need to revisit these questions time and again.

1. Are you experiencing any physical illnesses reflective of the root chakra?
   a. How do your legs feel? Heavy, flexible, tight, achy?

    b. Do you feel supported by your lower body or a weakness in the knees or ankles?

    c. Do you have inflammation in your body? Examples are hypertension, varicose veins, allergies, or arthritis.

    d. Do you have an autoimmune illness? Examples are MS, lupus, or Crohn's.

    e. Do you struggle with digestive issues?

    f. Are you constantly struggling with your weight?

    g. Do you have osteoporosis?

    h. Have you been challenged with adrenal fatigue?

2. Are you aware of your physical body's current needs? Could you explain them if you needed to?

3. Are you anxious or depressed?

4. Are you everything to everyone but yourself?

5. Do you catch colds frequently? Do you feel like your immunity is low?

6. Can you be impulsive and aggressive in nature?

7. Do you prefer routine and have trouble dealing with any change in plans?

8. Do you feel stagnant in life, working on autopilot?

9. Do you crave animal-based foods?

10. Do you crave the sweet flavor?

CHAPTER 7

SACRAL CHAKRA: FLOWING FREELY WITH LIFE

SACRAL CHAKRA

Essence: Creativity and Emotions
Life Lesson: Letting Go of Control
Physical: Kidneys/Bladder/Reproductive
Food: Fats and Oils
Flavor: Salty
Color: Orange

The sacral chakra is where your creativity lies, both in the physical sense of procreation and in the sense of ideas that you are able to manifest into form. The sacral chakra, physical in nature like the root chakra, is located directly below the navel.

Essential Nature: Creativity and Emotions

The sacral chakra is the home of your emotions and where you give meaning to experiences and learn what your desires, passions, and dreams are. Here lies your potential to create anything. Through emotions, the link between body and mind, your ideas can begin their path to physical reality. The right to feel your emotions is at the heart of the sacral chakra energy. Many of us have been programmed to believe that emotional expression is a sign of weakness and so have taken on the emotional climate of parents and other authoritative figures in our lives.

Dr. Candace Pert, in her audiotape *The Body Is Your Subconscious Mind,* explained the importance of emotional integrity, that no emotion, even anger, is without purpose and that all are healthy to experience. Those who choose to hold their emotions in, playing the stoic role, are the first to experience illness. Every experience you have has an emotional element, making your emotions the link to having a full experience in life. The challenge comes in how you choose to express your emotions: Will you have integrity and express yourself honestly, or will you choose to use emotion as a way to control and manipulate?

Knowing you have a right to feel and finding your emotional identity make it possible for you to experience and form intimate bonds and be sexually expressive with healthy boundaries. This chakra is all about relationships. The theme of control plays a role in any relationship you may have with another.

At this sacral chakra level of consciousness, survival is still a major factor influencing choices. We continue to look for predictability and safety. Stepping into a controlling role helps to combat the ultimate fear of the sacral chakra—losing control. Control can happen in different forms of energy currency. It happens through physical domination or psychological manipulation of another, how you use your sexuality, your relationship with money, and your emotional responses to get a desired outcome.

Sex, money, and volatile emotions are all currencies that can be used in ways to obtain external power. Physical rape or assault is a violation of a person's entire energy system. Rape also happens on an energetic level through the use of manipulation and continuous sabotaging of someone's dreams and autonomy. Here in the sacral chakra, it becomes about asking what your life values are, peeling back a layer and going beyond the choice to the underlying motivation behind it. Your morals reside in this energy center, asking things such as "What's your paying price?" and "Will you sacrifice or sell yourself for a measure of survival or safety?"

Life Lesson: Letting Go of Control

The sacral chakra energies are linked to the Water element, which is about continuous transformation, going with the flow of life, and embracing life's inevitable changes. Most of us, however, strive to grasp onto life, find some permanence, and make the big decisions that will hopefully lead us to the degree of safety we seek. We find ourselves full of habits and hardwired behaviors, and everything about life is known in detail.

At one point, my approach to life was supported by multiple calendars, Post-it notes, and preplanning a year to two in advance. The problem is when I tried to control every aspect of my life, I discouraged spontaneity and failed to let life in. This diminished the opportunities and experiences available to me. Perhaps you can relate. Life is so much bigger than what we can even imagine with players in our experiences we haven't yet met. Going with the flow allows the Universe to help us create what we need, presenting the people and circumstances necessary to take us to the next level of our evolution.

When you are balanced in the sacral chakra, you are willing to go with this flow of change. Continuously using your creative energy, you have a desire to express and manifest things into the physical world. By becoming open to life's adventures, there is no longer a need to predict or micromanage every outcome. Operating from integrity and establishing clear and healthy boundaries makes it possible to remain open, be expressive, and when necessary, respond with resolve.

Getting caught in a cycle of conditioned habits disrupts our life force, and life becomes stagnant. This stagnancy can be felt physically through body stiffness, lower back pain, chronic constipation and congestion as well as reproductive issues such as endometriosis, low libido, PMS, and hot flashes. Thinking becomes habitual and routine, and you may develop strict rules of how things should be, becoming quick to label people, things, or situations as good or bad.

Physiology of the Sacral Chakra

The sacral chakra is linked to our physiology through the kidneys, bladder, large intestines, and reproductive system.

Your kidneys, weighing around five ounces each, are an active organ using 25 percent of your blood at rest and almost 20–25 percent of your oxygen. They assist in an oxygen-carrying capacity, blood cleansing, and production of urine to the bladder. They also aid in the production of hormones that regulate blood pressure and assist in bone strength and the making of red blood cells. In TCM, the kidneys are believed to store your life essence and house your willpower, representing your overall stamina. Together these organs are transforming and transporting body fluids, acting as the regulators of water metabolism in the body.

In TCM, the sacral chakra is linked to the Water element of nature, so understanding the body's water regulation is important to keeping this chakra balanced. Water makes up 65 percent of an adult's weight and is essential for life. So many people walk around with their large coffees in their hands, admittedly dehydrated. Water is not only 90 percent of your blood; it is part of chemical structures that form all cells, tissues, and organs. Your brain, heart, lungs, and muscles are over 70 percent water—even your bones are 30 percent water. It's the body's universal solvent and a transport vehicle for nutrients and wastes. Without proper hydration, your blood becomes viscous and the delivery of oxygen to your cells is slowed down, which is a major cause of feeling sluggish and tired.

Water cushions and lubricates your joints, so it's not a coincidence that you feel bone stiffness and arthritic-type aches and pains when you are dehydrated. Water lubricates the digestive tract, respiratory tract, and all tissues that need to be moistened to function properly. The list goes on and on. Incorporating high-water-content foods will be part of the upcoming nutritional strategies to nurturing the sacral chakra.

The large intestine is also linked to the sacral energies. The large intestine receives wastes from the small intestine, absorbing the fluids and excreting the waste. Our digestive system, stomach, and small intestine extract nutrients from food, and the large intestine removes what we do not need.

But our understanding of the sacral chakra goes much deeper than the mechanics of digestion. In Eastern teachings, your large intestine is an indicator of your ability to move on from circumstances that no longer serve you, from negative thinking to unhealthy behavior patterns, whether you express your emotions or hold them in, and how well you flow with change. The large intestine energy meridian includes the head, sinuses, and lower back, so it's not a coincidence that constipation leads to feeling congested, with sinus pressure and morning lower back stiffness.

The reproductive system, as part of the energies of creation, is also linked to the sacral chakra. Wishing to bring another life into the world along with the general essence to create in the physical world is part of the reproductive process. It is a space to connect with your femininity and masculinity, welcoming both aspects into the full expression of who you are. Sexuality, intimate unions, and the openness to sensual pleasures does impact the energy flow to this area. When these capacities are unbalanced, such issues as impotence, infertility, menstrual difficulties, frigidity, or promiscuity will surface.

Food and the Sacral Chakra

Using a blend of Eastern teachings and modern science, we will explore how particular foods and liquids—water, fats, salty foods, and orange- and blue-colored foods—impact energy flow to the sacral chakra, initiating and enhancing your experience of flowing freely with life.

Water. Hydration sits at the top of the list of nutritional strategies for the sacral chakra. Your body works more efficiently when hydrated, noticeable in your energy levels, the lubrication around joints, and the health of your digestive system. As mentioned above, the large intestines, corresponding to the ability to let go, are enmeshed in the sacral energies. Staying hydrated along with consuming high-fiber foods helps food wastes pass more easily through the digestive tract with a faster transit time.

Consider adding high-water-content foods to your diet. These foods are fruits and vegetables, many ranging from being 80–95 percent water content. Not only are you staying hydrated, but these foods contain health-supportive phytonutrients, vitamins, minerals, and fiber. Consider including beets, broccoli, cabbage, cauliflower, bell peppers, carrots, green peas, radishes, celery, cucumbers, and tomatoes into your dietary pattern.

Fats. As explored in stage 1, fats are an essential nutrient with many physiological and health-promoting roles. Resist getting caught up in the mainstream thinking that fat is synonymous with weight gain. Eating fat does not make you fat.

Fats and oils are the perfect representation of the sacral chakra's duality. Fats can be free-flowing and flexible, as in a polyunsaturated fat, or stable and solid, as in saturated fat. Saturated fats, as in clarified butter or coconut oil, provide a grounding effect. Their stability is reflected by their slower vibrational essence, the fat creating a sense of security and fullness after a meal. Eating a diet high in saturated fat with a heavy use of butter or daily consumption of land animal flesh can be detrimental long term to your immunity.

Polyunsaturated fats, especially those omega-3 fatty acids, currently getting their fifteen minutes of fame, have different energetic and physiological properties than the saturated fats. Omega-3 fats help to enhance your immunity and counteract many inflammatory processes. Polyunsaturated fats can be found in flaxseeds, pumpkin seeds, walnuts, soybeans, and wild-caught fish such as salmon or halibut.

Fish, in addition to being a quality fat source, carry the energetic essence of water. Having an aversion to eating fish provides a deeper message about your sacral chakra. Ask yourself where or what in your life are you resisting? Can you let life in and release your need for control? Does this mean never eat any saturated fats? No! Let's keep things in context. All fats have value. It comes down to quantity and the ratio between the different types of fats. If you want to begin climbing the chakras in consciousness, consider emphasizing the more flexible fats and oils (polyunsaturated found in plant food) in your dietary pattern. These food choices will be reflected in your own vibrational essence.

Salty Flavor and Moistening Foods. As you learned in stage 1, flavors have thermal natures and a nurturing relationship to particular organs in the body. The salty flavor, linked to the Water element of nature, fortifies the kidneys and bladder of the sacral chakra.

The salty flavor draws energy inward and down, providing grounding qualities. You may feel a craving for salt when you don't feel safe or in control. Salt also has a moistening effect, alleviating internal dryness that can show up in muscle, joint, and mental inflexibilities. The salty flavor can help remove stagnation. However, this doesn't mean to start shaking lots of salt on all your meals!

I recommend cooking with a high-quality sea salt, one that is created from the evaporation of seawater with all its beneficial trace minerals intact. Seaweeds, tamari soy sauce, fermented miso, sardines, barley, and millet are additional food sources with the salty flavor. If you realize you have a dry constitution, are frequently thirsty, have dry skin, and struggle with constipation, then add foods with moistening qualities into your dietary pattern.

In addition to the salty ones just mentioned, start incorporating soybeans, almonds, mushrooms, walnuts, navy beans, radishes, tempeh, and cooked pears or apples. If you take the salt and moistening foods to an extreme, or consume too much oily and fatty food, get some cooked bitter leafy greens into your diet, like watercress, endive, arugula, and escarole.

Orange and Blue Foods. The sacral chakra, like the root chakra, vibrates at a relatively slow frequency. The sacral energies are still physical in nature and still about survival and security. The color orange resonates with the sacral chakra, making orange foods as well as the complementary color of blue an additional supporter of drawing more energy flow to nourish and heal at the level of the sacral chakra. Be mindful of your attraction or aversion to these colors, since you are most likely to gravitate toward colors, or vibrational frequencies, that reflect areas in your life needing your attention.

The recommendation of eating a rainbow diet continues as we add more diversity to your plate. Consider adding such foods as carrots, squash, sweet potatoes, mangos, apricots, papaya, and pumpkin to your dietary pattern. The complementary blue color resonates also with an upper chakra, the throat chakra, which is nurtured through eating high-water-content fruits and incorporating soups into your diet. In a later chapter on the throat, you will see how emotions of the sacral chakra impact your self-expression in the world. Connection after connection, you are coming closer to discovering your authentic self.

Strategies for Balance

When it comes to dietary changes for sacral balance, it will require some change to your food choices. If the food suggestions I am making have you instantly responding with "No, I don't like that," ask how open you really are to eating something new. It's easy to stay true to form and remain within our comfort zone, making no real commitment to change.

Perhaps a part of the sacral chakra's essence is resonating with you, specifically the control needs, difficulty with emotional expression, and reproductive struggles. The sacral chakra asks you to become more flexible in life, moving up from the root chakra that has you rooted like a tree. You are still seeking the quality of firm grounding at this level, but adding another element, the capacity to feel and have full emotional experiences. The sacral chakra brings awareness to emotional attachments, including your relationship to others and even your relationship with food, so you can make choices that keep you balanced.

You may initially choose to be mindful of your hydration, incorporating a new vegetable into your diet, sharing a meal with a neighbor, or observing how your emotions govern your food choices. Sometimes, it simply means getting out of a diet rut. I've met many who ate the same breakfast every morning for years and even had the same dinners on specific days of the week. It's time to expand the list of foods to include a variety of foods, even ones you have never tried before.

The sacral energies are about gracefully flowing with life's inevitable change, and a great way to do this is to literally get in the water. Go for a swim, sit at the edge of the ocean and let the waves splash up on your legs, or take a long bath. Get connected to the Water element. Dancing also helps, getting you moving to loosen up the hips and experience some play. And don't worry if you have no rhythm like me. No one is really paying that much attention. I take Tai Chi classes at the local gardens and call it my "dance class with the Universe." You can even take a Zumba dance class in the water or find a dance class nearby. Partner dancing adds another element of connection and relationship.

Consider letting life in! You won't be disappointed.

Sacral Chakra Strategies for Balance

- Incorporate sea animal and plant-based protein sources.
- Use mono- and polyunsaturated fats in your diet: olive oil, flaxseeds, hemp, and pumpkin seeds.
- Eat salty flavor foods in the form of sea salt, seaweed, tamari, barley, or millet.
- Stay hydrated through water consumption and high-water-content foods.
- Eat orange-colored foods.
- Stay committed to the changes you agreed to make with your relationship with food.
- Get out of your routine of eating the same foods. Try something new at least once a week.
- Be playful about preparing meals—it doesn't need to be a chore.
- Share a meal with someone who you wouldn't normally eat with.

Self-Reflective Questions

Understanding your sacral chakra begins with awareness. Take a moment to contemplate the following questions and expand your awareness of your current life circumstances and beliefs. The sacral chakra is about letting go of what no longer serves you. Can you acknowledge where your resistance to change may be coming from? Return to these questions over time. With every touch of change you invite into your life, your nutritional needs will change, too.

1. Are you experiencing any physical illnesses reflective of the sacral chakra?
   a. Do you have any reproductive illnesses or dysfunction (impotence, infertility, fibroids, endometriosis)?
   b. Do you get frequent bladder infections?

   c. Are you susceptible to kidney stones or have any other kidney disease?

   d. Do you struggle with chronic constipation? With the addition of sinus pressure and congestion?

   e. Are you prone to colon polyps?

   f. Do you have arthritis or complain of frequent stiff joints?

   g. Do you have chronic lower back pain?

2. Do you feel stagnant in life?

3. What are you emotionally attached to (people, money, food)?

4. When is the last time you created something? (It can be as simple as a meal.)

5. Are you able to express your emotions with integrity?

6. Do you have any addictions (money, sex, alcohol, food) that need to be acknowledged?

7. Are you an emotional eater, using food to distance yourself from your feelings?

8. Do you have an aversion to fish?

9. Do you crave salty foods?

10. Do you often find yourself dehydrated?

CHAPTER 8

Solar Plexus Chakra: Finding Inner Courage

SOLAR PLEXUS CHAKRA

Essence: Inner Courage and Personal Power
Life Lesson: Self-Esteem and Intuition
Physical: Digestive System
Food: Carbohydrates
Flavor: Bitter
Color: Yellow

The solar plexus chakra, located right above the waist, joins the root and sacral chakras in their unified focus on our relationship to the physical world. As you've seen, your root chakra grounds you in a sense of belonging and security within your community and home, and your sacral chakra connects you to others in one-on-one, personal relationships. Now the solar plexus focuses on how you relate to yourself—your self-esteem—and your ability to project your deepest truths into the world with courage and confidence.

You will see that as you climb up the ladder of the chakra system, your consciousness expands beyond the physical to becoming more spiritual in your focus.

Essential Nature: Inner Courage and Personal Power

The solar plexus chakra is the seat of your will, where you focus on developing a sense of self-identity. It is the home to our personal power and having the strength of character to step out of conformity, stop living as others expect, and learn to stand on our own.

The solar plexus chakra is linked to the Fire element in TCM. Fire is about transformation, making it an agent of change. Fire awakens through its passionate, outward energy, providing the opportunity for a rebirth, a chance to reinvent yourself this time around in a way that is aligned with your personal truth. When you feel that fire inside you, you thrive on activity, are eager to take on new adventures, and feel fed the nourishment necessary to prepare for change. This comes from a balanced energy flow to the solar plexus. You can stand your own ground; you're ambitious and want to discover your authentic self. It takes a lot of inner courage and strength to peel back the layers of who you are, and the Fire element is the essence that awakens you to act.

Life Lessons: Self-Esteem and Intuition

The lesson of self-esteem available at the solar plexus chakra is a crucial lesson needed to begin living life aligned with your authentic self. It's at this level where inner courage and personal power are developed, as you start to make choices from your own inner guidance, regardless of outside opinion.

Is this easy to do? Not in the beginning. I do assure you that with every step you take, however minor, to reclaim your life as yours, you will reap the benefits. Will people in your life have critical reactions and even try to intervene? Of course! But that's the exact fear and authority you are wishing to unplug from.

I can share it took me until close to my forties to begin reinventing myself and living my authentic life. This was a major life challenge for me. I found that it's only when you see your own value that you can begin to make healthy decisions aligned with your authentic self. After all, the solar plexus chakra is all about transformation. This is the time when we awaken and act. For each choice you make that calls upon your inner courage, the stronger and higher your energetic vibration will become. You will be amazed at how the circumstances and experiences in your life will be reflective of this.

I was aware of my gut responses for a long time but had never followed through on them. I was ruled by fear and wasn't going to take the chance if there were no guarantees. So instead, I constantly ignored my intuition, did the opposite, and then wanted to kick myself for not acting on my intuition. Sound familiar?

A major lesson of the solar plexus chakra is learning to trust your gut intuition. In TCM, the small intestine is the source of your gut feelings and intuition. "Go with your gut" is an expression that points to the fact that we are multisensory beings, moving past our basic five senses to include a sixth sense of intuition. This includes those hunches you feel when there's no conscious logic or rationalizing going on—you just know. The more intuitive you are, the more connected you are to your body and the less you are hiding away in your intellect, listening to the incessant fear-based chatter of the mind.

Finally, I decided to try trusting my intuition for minor, non-life-altering decisions. I felt this sense of confidence and inner joy each time I chose more intuitively. I started to feel playful about life and a tad rebellious, and I liked it. My self-esteem started to grow, and I began making choices aligned with my inner self. I was certainly rocking the boat.

Everyone has intuition; it's just commonly ignored or is operating outside their level of awareness. However, the more you become aware of it, the more you are developing your own inner guidance and the ultimate gift of being human—your free will.

You have the right to be who you are without fear or judgment. As you trust your intuition more, your overall level of awareness is heightened, shifting your perception of reality. Billions of bits of information come flooding into our brains every second, and only a tiny amount makes it into our conscious awareness. Relying on intuition actually shifts your sense of self, and you begin to vibrate at a higher level of consciousness, one that is palpable to others as it manifests in your presence.

When you are balanced in the solar plexus chakra, you have strong self-esteem and self-respect. You have a presence that exudes confidence with an inspiring flair. You are approachable, playful, and smile more often. You can see the humor in things. When the energy flowing to the solar plexus is strong, you make choices in life based on your most authentic self and risk disapproval for the integrity of your own truth. The more you rely on inner courage and guidance, the less people will be able to control you. Their attempts fall to the wayside because you no longer attach your self-worth to their opinions, criticisms, or expectations. This is one of the most freeing experiences you can ever have as a human being.

The lessons of the solar plexus chakra are challenging ones that many people spend a lifetime working on. Operating from your inner courage while yearning for connection with others can make life feel like an uphill battle. It's the fears of rejection that seem like a constant struggle.

Time spent discovering your personal power is one of the most challenging and rewarding investments you could possibly make in this lifetime. And the bonus is that for every choice you make toward your authentic self, you are inspiring others to do the same. The ultimate gift of the solar plexus chakra is giving your unconditional support to another. Now that's inspiring!

Physiology of the Solar Plexus Chakra

The vibrational energy of this center stimulates and influences the upper parts of the digestive system and its organs, including the small intestine, stomach and spleen, liver and gallbladder, and pancreas.

Small Intestine. The small intestine is responsible for absorbing nutrients from food and filtering out the impurities before nutrients are sent to the liver for distribution to the body. The small intestine is your body's filter, analogous to the filter of your awareness allowing only certain opinions, beliefs, and judgments to enter your consciousness. When the lining of the small intestine is compromised from poor diet or chronic stress, a leaky gut arises. In this condition, impure foods and other toxins can overtax the liver and spill over into the blood and lymphatic system, leading to an overburdened immune system. If this becomes a chronic state, it creates the foundation for inflammatory issues such as arthritis, autoimmune illness, asthma, depression, anxiety, overall digestive dysfunction, food intolerances, and even weight gain.

Without an effective working filter, every word of criticism and disapproval gets absorbed into your being. Don't be surprised if you are left with unpredictable digestive responses, some painful and others filled with embarrassment and shame. Since the digestive system is the center of transformation where energy and nutrients are extracted from food, digestion is going to be the major physiological link to the solar plexus chakra.

Stomach and Spleen. The stomach and spleen play a major role in your overall digestive function and immunity, as well as in you feeling centered, as described in the chapter on the root chakra. Balance in these organs allows you to begin making choices aligned with your inner truth. The root and solar plexus chakras work very closely together, so there is no surprise a shared physiological connection exists.

Although we can look at each chakra to understand its nature, the physiological correlations, and underlying life lessons, we also need to take a step back and recognize that all these chakras are working in a holistic, synergistic fashion on an even larger scale. You'll find some chakras overlap, relate to varying degrees, influence, and even hinder other energies depending on what is happening at the present time.

With that in mind, let's look at the stomach and spleen. As mentioned earlier, the digestive system operates through what are called warm transactions, meaning food needs to become a warm soup, a little warmer than core temperature, for proper digestion to occur. To extract energy and nutrients from food, the most beneficial way to consume food is cooked. Cooked food initiates the digestion process and maintains the integrity of the stomach and spleen.

Does this mean you should never eat raw food? No—there are no absolutes about food and eating. It all depends on the context. If you are struggling with digestive dysfunction such as acid reflex, gas, bloating, constipation, or you have signs of inflammation as in arthritis, asthma, or heart disease, then raw and cold food are not your friends. The same applies if you have a known autoimmune disease, such as Crohn's or IBS, or you are experiencing chronic fatigue, have energy slumps daily, or are on your way to becoming a diabetic.

If you have a robust digestive system; enjoy immune, digestive, and emotional stability; feel a fire burning inside you; and walk with a presence of inner courage; then incorporating some raw food may work in your diet—especially during the hot summers. The concern with consuming raw or cold food is that it impedes the transformational processes of digestion. Cold contradicts the warm soup we need to create for efficient digestion, and raw creates a dampness that weakens the spleen, leading over time to stagnant energy, inflammatory responses, and weight gain, particularly in the abdominal area.

The food marketing world urges you to consume juices and smoothies to provide a concentrated liquid meal packed full of ingredients. It's quick and easy, taking minimal effort. And it's true, if you look at a blender full of leafy greens, veggies, fruits, seeds, and nuts, there's no debate that such a drink is loaded with health-supportive nutrients. The question becomes how does this cold, raw, and concentrated food impact your digestion?

The truth is, it's not what you eat that makes a difference, it's what you can absorb and assimilate. Would you eat each of the foods that you put in your morning smoothie if you didn't put them in a blender and drink it? In other words, would you eat those same foods on a plate every day? Probably not. When you consume all those fruits and vegetables in a raw and concentrated form, you are taking in the essence, not just the nourishment of all that food. Inside the body, that translates to the formation of dampness, so say hello to excess phlegm, a sluggish energy state, and the quick weight gain that comes with it.

Raw foods, especially when part of your regular dietary pattern, regardless of their caloric intake, are damaging to the digestive and metabolic processes. If weight loss is a goal, it takes finding your ground and healing your digestive system to experience long-term results. Those daily morning smoothies and raw lunch salads could be hindering your progress.

Many raw enthusiasts will tell you that consuming raw foods maintains the integrity of the enzymes, making the food alive with all its nutrients intact. But this is where the concept of context comes into play. There is a difference between gross income and net profit. It's important that we view the net absorption of a food instead of its static gross estimation. The number of nutrients measured in raw food in a laboratory does not represent the post-digestive absorption of that food.

The primatologist Rich Wrangham writes in *Catching Fire* how cooking made us human. We are the only species that cooks our food.

The result is a smaller, more efficient digestive system to support us as creative thinkers with a large frontal lobe, not spending most of our time chewing and digesting the wild boar we caught that day. Contrary to the advice of popular diets, we are not cavemen anymore. We're Homo sapiens, evolved human beings, and cooking our food has played a role in shifting our evolution to make us more conscious and intelligent.

Liver and Gallbladder. The liver performs hundreds of functions, from distributing energy and blood to cells to managing detoxification and immune responses. When your liver is functioning well, you have a relaxed and playful demeanor. When the body's energy flow becomes obstructed, stagnation develops, and you are likely to bottle up emotions and have outbursts of anger. Physically, digestive issues surface, and you start to feel heavy and sluggish, unmotivated, and at the same time impatient.

The gallbladder, the organ responsible for storing bile and digesting fats and affected by the health of the liver, is also energetically the organ of making decisions. When you are balanced within the solar plexus energies, feeling your inner Fire essence and able to take action, your gallbladder is functioning well. It's when you lack assertiveness and sit in a space of indecisiveness without healthy emotional expression that troubles arise.

Pancreas. The pancreas has two main functions: to release enzymes that assist in the digestive process and to produce hormones such as insulin and glucagon to maintain blood sugar levels. It is the pancreas's job to detect blood sugar levels, whether high or low, and respond by either removing or releasing glucose from the bloodstream. When the regulation of blood sugar is chronically impaired, either from the pancreas not producing enough insulin or the cells not responding, it creates the onset of diabetes.

The energetic side of the pancreas, linked to the spleen, carries the emotion of worry. Those who worry all the time have almost an obsessive quality about detail, are perfectionists at heart, and make most of their decisions from the intellect. Behind all of that is usually some serious resentment.

Food and the Solar Plexus

The solar plexus chakra is about transformation and energy production. The preferred fuel to energize the body comes in the form of carbohydrate, in its simplest form as glucose, especially when accompanied by fiber-rich foods. Bitter flavors and yellow-colored foods further enhance your experience of solar plexus empowerment.

Carbohydrates. As discussed earlier, carbohydrates have received a bad reputation and are continuously blamed for an endless list of health problems. But just like all the rest, protein and fat included, carbs play a role in a larger process. Remember—the body works in a holistic system with parts connecting, influencing, and stimulating every other part. Biochemical pathways are shared among many physiological processes, called redundant signaling, leaving no condition ever the cause of one chemical, hormone, food, and in this case, nutrient.

Carbohydrates, or glucose, is the preferred fuel source of the body. It provides the energy for you to think, breathe, and exercise as well as all the involuntary biological reactions that give you the gift of life. The functions of your heart, kidneys, and nervous system operate through the energy extracted from the chemical bonds of glucose.

The question becomes, What is your definition of a carbohydrate? I'm referring to the food provided by nature, such as legumes, grains, fruits, and vegetables. Forget the bakery sweets, the soft yet crunchy-on-the-outside Italian breads and cream puffs. I call those items processed foods, and they are high in concentrated sugars, as well as fats. Take processed foods out of the category of carbohydrates, and it will make eating strategies for the solar plexus, specifically the management of your energy levels and physical weight, much more attainable.

Particular benefits of carbohydrates relevant to the solar plexus chakra are their health-promoting phytonutrient content and the regulation of blood sugar levels and digestive health. These phytonutrients have immune-boosting and health-protective qualities that have been found to impact health all the way to the genetic level. We touched upon this in chapter 1 on physical properties of food. This makes your everyday food choices a strong influence on whether you will project health or struggle with disease. Emphasizing a plant-based diet will assure that these antioxidant, anti-inflammatory and disease-preventing compounds are available to you.

Fiber. Along with being a valuable supply of phytonutrients, vitamins, minerals, and even protein, carbohydrates contain fiber. Fiber plays a part in regulating blood sugar levels and maintaining a healthy digestive system and comes in two forms: soluble and insoluble. Soluble fibers, found in fruits, vegetables, beans, and grains such as oatmeal and barley, delay nutrient transit time through the digestive system. This slows down glucose absorption and prevents at burst of glucose into the blood that can be especially difficult for those with metabolic dysfunction and insulin resistance and are overweight or challenged with diabetes. Think of it as a slow drip from a faucet instead of turning the faucet on full blast. The body requires a steady, continuous supply of glucose to feed the brain, supply energy, keep the digestive system fit, and yes, manage weight.

It's tempting to turn the glucose faucet on full blast with a large coffee and bag of candy. Instead, consider reaching for fiber-rich foods such as berries, pears, apples with the skin, leafy greens, lentils, and peas. Adding insoluble fibers along with staying hydrated helps to ease elimination and supports the health of the colon. The insoluble fibers, found in the structural walls of the skin of corn kernels, celery strings, and bran, stimulate the digestive tract, strengthening its musculature while speeding up the time putrefied food remains in the intestines.

For everyone, it is important to prevent and alleviate chronic constipation, not only for digestive health but for overall health and the risk reduction of colon cancers.

Bitter and Sour Flavors. The bitter flavor corresponds to the Fire element, becoming the primary flavor of the solar plexus energies but not to the exclusion of others. In keeping with the holistic view of the body, each flavor influences and supports all the others in a well-orchestrated dance. The bitter flavor has contracting and cooling qualities, helps remove dampness, and has eliminating qualities that assist the liver in the detoxification process.

Consider adding romaine, watercress, escarole, chard, scallions, celery, and quinoa to your dietary pattern. Along with keeping a strong flavor of bitter in your diet while addressing your solar plexus energies, add some sour flavor. Sour stimulates energy flow to the liver and gallbladder. It's essential to keep blood and energy moving, so you don't experience stagnation that can show up as irritability, anger, bloating, and constipation. Add some lemons, limes, apple cider vinegar, and sauerkraut in small quantities to your dietary pattern.

Yellow or Purple Foods. The color yellow resonates with the solar plexus chakra, making yellow foods, as well as the complementary color of purple, an additional support for drawing more energy flow to nourish and heal this level. Consider adding yellow bell peppers, summer squash, chickpeas, bananas, pineapple, millet, corn, and yellow beets to your dietary pattern.

The complementary color of purple resonates also with the third eye chakra, which complements the solar plexus chakra. Eating purple foods, such as grapes, blackberries, eggplant, plums, and purple kale will enhance the vibration of this chakra's energy while supplying antioxidant and anti-inflammatory protective qualities.

Strategies for Balance

The solar plexus chakra is about taking action. No more talking about what you know you need to do. It's time to connect with your inner courage and use your will to move forward. This chakra draws attention to spring-cleaning time, a time to eliminate irritants and triggers in the form of people and situations as well as food intolerances and begin with a fresh start. Keep your dietary pattern light and bright, making sure not to eat in excess, and keep the body moving. It's time to get your filters working effectively, so you can begin discovering your authentic self and feeling your value.

If you don't cook for yourself or your family, learning to cook is a key step to take to demonstrate your willingness to be proactive in shifting your relationship with food. You do not need to go to culinary school, cook fancy four-course meals, or strive to be the next contestant on *Chopped*. Learning simple culinary techniques, from knife skills to cooking methods, is all you need. There's millions of recipes on the internet at your fingertips—give one a try!

Public cooking classes on knife skills, health-supportive cooking, and exploring the traditional meals of other cultures are growing in numbers. As much as restaurant eating is filled with many pleasures, when you step into the kitchen yourself, you are claiming your power and hopping into the driver's seat of this transformational journey through food.

Physical exercise gives a positive boost to self-esteem. It's time to start an exercise program. Head to the gym for some strength-training exercises, sign yourself up to run a local 5K race, or join a yoga community. Get really daring and try a new exercise activity. How about stand-up paddleboarding?

Exercise not only enhances metabolic processes and boosts immunity but improves cognitive function and literally increases feelings of happiness. Consider exercising with others; this is a time not to isolate but to share who you are. Find a workout buddy or introduce yourself to someone in a class or group, bringing a social element into your exercise routine. It will be a lot more fun and more likely to keep you motivated.

Solar Plexus Chakra Strategies for Balance

- Emphasize a plant-based dietary pattern.
- Eat foods with the bitter flavor by incorporating more leafy greens.
- Add the sour flavor to assist in digestion and detoxification.
- Eat yellow- and purple-colored foods.
- Incorporate fermented foods to feed friendly bacteria of digestive tract.
- Stay hydrated while adding high-fiber foods to your diet.
- Eat the majority of meals cooked (but consider cold-natured foods in times of heat) for elevated Fire element and robust digestion.
- Take a proactive role and demonstrate personal responsibility by learning to cook.
- Be mindful not to overeat.
- Make yourself accountable and follow through with food changes.

Self-Reflective Questions

The solar plexus is about self-discovery. It's about having the courage to act. When we don't, we get stuck in that "all talk, no walk" rut. The questions of the solar plexus chakra ask you to think about what you want out of life, regardless of the opinions of others.

Sit with these questions below for as long as you need. A common reaction to imbalances at this level is to ignore, deny, or dodge straightforward questions because admitting you are aware of something means you are able to act, and you just might not be ready. Nevertheless, take a step and increase your awareness by considering answers to these questions:

1. Are you experiencing any physical illnesses reflective of the solar plexus chakra?
   a. Are you experiencing digestive distress (acid reflux, gas, bloating, constipation, diarrhea)?
   b. Do you have ulcers?
   c. Do you have a digestive illness (Crohn's, IBS, diverticulitis)?
   d. Do you struggle with chronic fatigue?
   e. Do you have diabetes?
2. Do you place a great deal of importance on achievement?
3. Can you follow through with a commitment you make, or do you find yourself in the "all talk, no walk" arena?
4. Can you say no when circumstances do not fit your understanding of integrity or needs?
5. Are you open to using your intuition as a guide?
6. Do you make life choices, starting with food choices, according to your needs and not according to others around you?
7. Do you find yourself being intrusive, often telling others what to eat when they haven't asked you?
8. Do you have energy slumps during the day, often reaching for quick energy foods or drinks?
9. Are you aware of how raw versus cooked foods impact your digestion, energy, and weight?

10. Do you struggle with your weight? Particularly in the abdominal region?

11. ***Bonus opportunity to self-reflect:*** Find a quiet space where you'll have no interruptions and answer this question: What do you want? Do not allow current life circumstances, limitations, or fears to influence your answer. Anything is possible. Write it down. Let it become a possibility in the Universe. Maybe it won't unfold exactly the way you want it to, but that doesn't mean the Universe isn't conspiring to respond in a way that is better than you could imagine.

CHAPTER 9

THE HEART CHAKRA: DISCOVER SELF-LOVE

HEART CHAKRA

Essence: Love
Life Lesson: Forgiveness
Physical: Heart/Lungs
Food: Leafy Greens
Flavor: Sour
Color: Green

You have now traveled through the three lower chakras to arrive at midpoint on the ladder of the human energy system, the heart chakra. Located at the center of your chest, the heart chakra's focus is on a more spiritual, less physical energy. Feeling and emotion become more dominant in your consciousness as you ascend the chakra ladder, elevating your vibrational energy and moving you toward a more liberating experience of life. Still grounded and feeling a connection to the Earth through your root chakra, you begin the self-inquiry to bring your attention to the theme of love.

Essential Nature: Love

Love is the strongest force in life, one that motivates and inspires us to engage the world with an open heart. This is the essential nature of the heart chakra, your energetic center that encompasses acceptance, gratitude, and compassion. In a space of love, altruistic acts become second nature and can be seen in the sheer kindness of smiling at a stranger. When you feel the presence of love, the lens through which you see life completely changes. Lending a helping hand occurs without hesitation, as you extend yourself naturally in compassion and caring for others as well as for yourself.

The heart chakra energies are largely focused on self-love. Self-love means you find acceptance and compassion for yourself, always understanding that you are a work in progress. When in the space of self-love, you are happy with yourself, enjoy your own company, and see the clear distinction between being alone and lonely. When the energy is freely flowing to the heart chakra, you feel fulfilled in your own presence. Love is the healing force, bringing with it inspiration and curiosity to ask personal questions about your own emotional needs, vulnerability limits, and willingness to be intimate with life.

Life Lessons: Forgiveness

The heart chakra's teaching is all about forgiveness. Forgiveness can be directed toward those who may have harmed you, but in many instances, it starts with forgiving yourself. Forgiving yourself and others can be one of the most challenging undertakings in this lifetime.

When you release yourself from a past hurt or even a choice you regret, taking the lesson that was delivered in the experience, it makes room for healing. Hanging on to a past hurt makes it impossible to grow and move forward. Life stops flowing, becomes stagnant, and starts to get reflected in your health. Stagnancy, or the inability to let go, obstructs blood circulation, as well as your life-force energy, or qi.

The heart chakra is filled with emotional energy and asks us once again to get out of our heads and into our bodies—to *feel*. When the heart chakra is unbalanced, you can easily hide out behind your intellect, rationalizing every decision you make. However, if you were to allow yourself to sit in intellect-only decisions, you might feel something lacking. Feeling allows for a full experience of life, the one that brings satisfaction and fulfillment. It is impossible to be intimate and vulnerable with others if we don't have that level of love for ourselves. Our boundaries then become blurred when clingy, manipulative, and codependent interactions dominating our relationships.

Physiology of the Heart Chakra

The organs that correlate to the heart chakra are the heart, lungs, and thymus gland. The arms are the physical structures that express the energy of the heart chakra through the act of touching.

Heart. The heart is more than a physical organ and has been referred to as the root of life. In many cultures and traditions, the heart has been understood to be vital to overall well-being. Physiologically, the heart controls the distribution and circulation of blood to the entire body. However, the heart is so much more than a pumping machine.

It may surprise you to know that the heart has its own intelligence system with electromagnetic forces much greater than the brain. The heart's magnetic field, bio-field, or aura radiates several feet out from the body, extending your essence beyond your physical skin. Your heart energy not only communicates with your brain but also can resonate in frequency with the heart/brain of whomever might be standing next to you. The heart is laced with every neuropeptide receptor, making it home to all emotions, and through a system of communication, it can stimulate and influence how you consciously make decisions. The heart is home to your soul.

The heart also has its own nervous system, is a hormonal gland, and generates a rhythmic coherence, whereas the rest of the body vibrates in harmony. Your heart's vibration, your capacity for self-love, impacts all of you—body, mind, and soul.

Lungs. Like the small intestine, the lungs facilitate an exchange between the outside and inner worlds, acting as an important part of the body's first line of immune defense. The lungs expand and disperse, breathing in air and distributing oxygen to the body. Breath is what makes you alive and is linked to every process in the body from blood circulation, sleep, and nervous system responses to the elimination of toxins. Breath enables you to speak by providing air, the force behind your voice, supporting your self-expression to the world. Breath is about give and take. With each breath, you have the opportunity to breathe out toxins and let go of beliefs and attitudes that no longer serve you, making room for new ones that do.

Are you aware of your breath right now? By observing your breath, you can see how well you can relax and find your center. This is because the rhythms of the breath govern the rhythms of the body. Whether you take in slow, deep breaths or ones more quick and shallow, your inner state is reflected in your breathing.

I struggled with shortness of breath for years, gasping for air and feeling like I couldn't get enough. My breathing was short and shallow, a sign of my underlying fear and anxiety. Relaxing was a tall feat. One of the major shifts in my life was adding breath work and meditation. What a powerful practice, one that is now part of my daily day.

Thymus Gland. The thymus gland, located behind the sternum in front of the heart, is associated with the heart and plays a role in immunity. It stimulates the production of white blood cells called T lymphocytes that help the body manage infections arising from bacteria, fungi, or viruses. The thymus gland is linked to our lymphatic system along with secreting hormones to regulate immunity. It does this by recognizing what is considered "you" and what is "not you," which is the essence of immunity. The thymus gland helps to protect against autoimmunity, a condition in which your own immune system attacks itself. Type 1 diabetes, Hashimoto's and Graves' disease, lupus, and rheumatoid arthritis are a few examples of autoimmunity disorders.

Arms. The arms, along with our shoulder blades and wrists, are extensions of the heart chakra through the capacity for touch. Touch is an important part of nurturing the heart energies, whether through a massage or simply the act of getting or giving a hug. The act of hugging releases a particular brain chemical, oxytocin, along with hormones serotonin and dopamine, all of which give a sense of comfort while decreasing feelings of loneliness. Levels of the stress hormone cortisol also drop because of nourishing touch, accompanied by a simultaneous reduction in blood pressure.

I know that even the thought of receiving a massage leaves many people uneasy. There's the thought, *I'm not sure how I feel about someone touching me.* If this resonates with you, my suggestion would be to begin with the people in your intimate circle and perhaps give a hello hug. A sincere hug! Not one of those where your backside is pointing down the street and there is a foot-wide gap between you. Get in there and give your friend a hug. Do you know how many times clients expressed their concern about whether people would hug them back? This is the classic sign of an unbalanced heart chakra, being desperate for connection but at the same time keeping distance from any real intimacy. For me it was a few pedicures, the discovery of Thai massages, and hugs from close friends that started me on my path to welcoming others into my personal space. These actions are all to practice receiving, finding the heart chakra's balance of give and take.

Heart Health, Anger, and Resentment

Wood, the element associated with the heart chakra, is aligned with the spring season, signaling new beginnings and growth. The Wood element is also linked to the functions of the liver and gallbladder, and while these organs are not vibrationally related to the heart chakra, their functions come into play through the Wood element to explain liver-associated anger and resentment that is behind many heart issues.

One of the liver's many jobs is keeping blood and qi flowing smoothly, reflected in its nickname commander of the blood. A continuous, unimpeded flow of qi is going to determine your health. Qi runs through the body in a precise pattern of two-hour intervals when specific organs are functioning at their peak. Qi flows through the organs of daily activity, like those of the digestive system, before turning inward to organs of restoration. The cycle ends between one and three in the morning, with qi flowing into the liver, which cleanses the blood, among other functions. The timing of early morning wake-ups is tied to the flow of qi, whether smooth or blocked, through that most active meridian. If you find yourself waking up at two thirty every morning because of a blocked flow of qi, recognize the possible internal stagnation and underlying buildup of resentment.

When the heart chakra is balanced and you are in a space of self-love, there is a healthy exchange of nutrients and removal of toxins. The energy you feel is expanding and rising, and you see life through an ambitious lens full of opportunities instead of obstacles When not in a space of self-love, especially if you feel your individuality has been compromised, stagnancy develops.

This can manifest as inflammation, interrupted sleep, and the emotions of frustration and anger..

Many have shared that after years of choosing to live a life of obligation, they developed a deep resentment and sadness for what their lives could have been. The anger can become so deep-seated that a struggle with insomnia and even the removal of the gallbladder, the organ of action, occurs.

Food and the Heart Chakra

Food for keeping the heart chakra balanced is going to emphasize immunity, circulation, and the support of the body's self-healing qualities. The intention is to eat foods that promote blood alkalinity, supply healthy fats, and keep sugar consumption at a minimum.

Alkalinizing Foods. In order for the body to function optimally, the blood needs to be slightly alkaline, a principle you learned about in chapter 1 in regard to the physical properties of food. To review, after digestion, plant foods leave what is called an alkaline ash. This allows for the oxygenation of the blood, which provides the most efficient environment for absorption of nutrients and removal of toxins. Foods that leave an acid ash acidify the blood and produce the opposite effect.

We can thank Dr. Otto Warburg, a biochemist and cell biologist who won the Nobel Prize in 1931, for proving just how important blood alkalinity is from his work on oxidation. His research showed that no disease exists in an oxygenated, alkaline environment. Further research has shown that well-oxygenated blood supports the self-healing capacity of the body, allowing for the growth, maintenance, and recycling of all cells. This recycling process regenerates the body to make it entirely new every decade.

It has been debated whether eating foods with an alkaline versus acidic effect in the body can improve the body's ability to repair, detoxify, and regenerate the cells. The chemistry involved needs a little unpacking: When speaking of alkaline and acid foods, the reference is to the effect on the blood after digestion, not the foods' composition. A food's composition outside the body is not an indicator of whether it is alkaline or acidic post-digestion. For example, lemons are acidic in composition; however, after digestion they form an alkaline ash.

When your blood is continuously exposed to an acidic ash and cannot maintain its alkalinity, the body rebalances by pulling calcium from your bones to neutralize the acidity, compromising your bones' structural integrity. Chronic exposure to an acidic ash has been further correlated to altered adrenal function, digestive dysfunction, inability to detoxify, and increase in inflammatory disease. This is a theory many may debate, yet one I think can be an attributing factor to finding a dietary pattern that provides nourishment and protection against inflammatory conditions in the body, whether heart disease, asthma, or osteoarthritis.

Healthy alkaline-forming foods include most fruits, vegetables, sea plants, fermented soy, herbal teas, and bone broth as well as the grains quinoa and millet. On the acidic-forming side, we find animal-based foods such as meat, eggs, dairy, beans, sugar, and gluten-based grains.

Current research continues to demonstrate the benefits of a plant-based diet, perhaps because plant foods tend to neutralize acidity, promoting an oxygenated environment. This is not to say you should avoid all acid-forming foods, which have other beneficial characteristics. The point is to recognize how foods respond differently when assimilated and rely on your observations when choosing the best dietary pattern for you.

Heart-Healthy Fats. Fats, a macronutrient of much controversy, actually play a beneficial role in heart health. It comes down to which fats, how they are prepared and how they fit into the context of the entire dietary pattern. Knowing avocados are healthy fats is not going to protect you from heart disease. There's more to the story, and I hope I can shed some light on the controversy around fats and the infamous cholesterol.

First, the type of fat that will demonstrate benefit to the heart chakra are those fats with anti-inflammatory pathways. All food, relative to their fat composition, travel different chemical pathways within the body, resulting in the production of hormonelike compounds called prostaglandins. Prostaglandins have the potential to relax blood vessels, improve circulation, lower blood pressure, and decrease inflammatory processes. Fats that produce these prostaglandins are found in nuts, seeds, cold-water fish, and the chlorophyll of dark leafy greens. Other fats, such as animal flesh, are pro-inflammatory, promoting platelet aggregation and elevated blood pressure but beneficial during fight-or-flight reactions.

Ideally, you want to incorporate foods rich in omega-3 fatty acid into your diet. The constituents of omega-3s are EPA (eicosapentaenoic acid) and DHA (docosahexaenoic acid). Both EPA and DHA are understood to reduce blood platelet stickiness and change the fluidity of cell membranes. This results in increased insulin receptor sensitivity, a good thing for your metabolism and for enhancing communication between cells.

My point is that fats can heal. Fats can protect you from heart disease. Fats can even regulate your blood sugar levels and impact your ability to lose weight. Seek out flaxseeds, hemp seeds, pumpkin seeds, salmon, halibut, and the chlorophyll-rich green parts of seaweeds and leafy greens for the essential fats that nurture the heart chakra.

Cholesterol. It has become a lucrative business to push cholesterol-lowering drugs and market foods low in cholesterol, but after billions of dollars spent yearly, there are still many myths that surround cholesterol's value.

First, cholesterol is essential to your health. Naturally occurring in the body, cholesterol produces hormones, vitamins, bile to digest fats, and is responsible for cell communication and cell membrane repair. Fats cannot be transported around freely in your bloodstream and must travel on a "protein bus" to get to and from cells. The two main buses are high-density lipoproteins (HDL) and low-density lipoproteins (LDL), or what have become known as the good and bad cholesterols. LDL transports cholesterol and other fats to cells, while HDL carries excess cholesterol and fats away from cells to the liver for elimination.

Cholesterol itself is not dangerous. It's only when cholesterol gets oxidized that problems arise. Oxidation happens when eating a diet heavy in animal products, dairy, sweets, and caffeinated beverages. Over time, these eating habits are acidic to the blood and pro-inflammatory. Blood vessel walls get injured through inflammation, and the cholesterol response to their repair begins an unwanted, unhealthy cascade of events.

Elevated cholesterol levels in the blood can also be due to too much stress. How many people say, "Stress is my middle name"? We can certainly feel functional in that we get through the day, but our bodies will still feel the effects. Since cholesterol is the precursor to many stress hormones, the more stress experienced, the higher the cholesterol rises in the bloodstream.

Remember—every cell in your body is an intelligent entity and responds to the truth, regardless of how you make it through the day. As much as cholesterol is a player in the inflammatory processes, it is by no means the cause; nor can reducing heart health to the actions of one molecule lead to successful prevention and treatment. Think of this: Aren't there more people on cholesterol-lowering drugs than ever before and heart disease is still America's number-one killer? Perhaps it's time to consider looking deeper into the underlying diet and lifestyle patterns that contribute to imbalances in the heart chakra energies.

Excessive Sweets. Excess sugar consumption becomes a big problem for heart chakra health because sugar can elevate cholesterol and triglycerides (amount of fat circulating in your blood), regardless of the amount of fat you consume. There is only so much sugar that can be stored in the liver and muscle. When storage has reached its capacity, the body will shift and use the remaining sugar as energy to the best of its ability. If the amount exceeds your energetic needs, then the body needs to handle the excess. How does it do that? The body breaks sugar down to use as energy, producing what is called 2 carbon acetates, or molecules of vinegar. These molecules of vinegar are actually the building blocks for cholesterol and saturated fats, so if they are not used as energy fast enough, the excess will be formed into cholesterol and fats. Having an excess of vinegar in the bloodstream is actually more toxic and detrimental than cholesterol and fats.

Isn't it amazing how everything is so interconnected? Excess sugar also does a number on the immune system and disrupts adrenal function, which then leads to increases in cholesterol along with cortisol, the stress hormone, and alters insulin receptor sensitivity. With that combination, weight management is almost impossible, along with a host of other undesirable effects.

In addition to sugar, be mindful not to consume other damp foods in excess. The heart chakra and root chakra, home of the Earth element, are intimately linked, making it essential to keep grounded while developing self-love.

Sour, Bitter, and Pungent Flavors. Eating a mixture of flavors is helpful to balancing the heart chakra energies. First add some sour foods, the flavor connected to the liver and gallbladder, to keep blood and energy flowing. Be conscious if you are feeling frustrated or know you have an underlying resentment. A little sour food a day can go a long way. Drink warm lemon water in the morning and eat a forkful of raw, unpasteurized sauerkraut.

The bitter flavor penetrates the heart and will drain dampness, plus it detoxifies from the consumption of excess sugar and/or animal-based foods. Think cabbage, broccoli, arugula, mustard greens, bok choy, and cauliflower. These bitter-tasting cruciferous vegetables have their own unique set of phytonutrients, making them jewels of health-promoting compounds. Pungent foods are also great for getting things moving, dispersing energy, and getting out of stagnant spaces. Pungent is about movement and flow. Add some garlic, onions, scallions, basil, ginger, and fennel to your meals.

Green or Red Foods. The color green resonates with the heart chakra, making green foods as well as the complementary color of red an additional supporter of drawing more energy flow to nourish and heal at this level of consciousness.

Green foods also carry the greenery and chlorophyll properties of the Wood element. Chlorophyll aids in regeneration, immunity, blood cleansing, and oxygenation. Consider adding arugula, asparagus, collard greens, broccoli, avocado, brussels sprouts, and kiwi fruit to your dietary pattern.

The complementary color of red, the vibration of the root chakra, underscores how these two chakras are intimately connected. Quite often challenges in the heart chakra have a correlation to the group mind and yearning for connection. The red pigment of foods such as beets, adzuki beans, tomatoes, strawberries, watermelon, and apples can enhance the vibration of the heart chakra's energies. Beets have been known in ancient traditions to have many healing benefits, from providing a sense of grounding to purifying the blood, while adzuki beans are known as the legume of the heart. Let these foods help you find your center so you can ask and answer the question of what makes you happy, an inquiry that puts you on the road to healing any heart chakra imbalances.

Strategies for Balance

Eating for heart chakra balance involves the nutrients in your food but also the nourishing experience of dining and mealtime. You are balancing an emotional energy, so all your thoughts, words, and actions around meals should be done with the vibration of love.

Take the time to be a part of your healing process through positive action toward your food choices. Make the time to shop, prepare, and store foods that best serve you, so they are continuously available. Make yourself a priority. This is the time to cook for yourself, even if it's only for you alone. Show some self-love and demonstrate that you are worth the effort. Intimacy with others won't happen if you don't have love for yourself.

Another strategy is to share meals with others and appreciate their presence in your life. While you're in the kitchen, put some music on. Humming or toning deepens your breath, reduces heart rate, and improves your overall sense of well-being. Go ahead and sing and hum your way through putting together recipes. Remember a happy chef creates loving meals!

In terms of physical exercise, the cardio-respiratory system loves movement that gets the blood and lymph flowing throughout the body. A great way to do that is through aerobic exercise. Aerobic exercise is an activity that uses large muscle groups in a rhythmic fashion. Examples are jogging, cycling, swimming, or even the elliptical trainer at your gym.

Aerobic exercise strengthens your heart, improves lung capacity, enhances immunity, shifts your metabolism, and even vasodilates blood vessels to lower your blood pressure. People who are part of a consistent exercise program also feel a heightened sense of self; their confidence is elevated, and they become motivated to make other changes in their lives. The key is the intensity.

In a visit to my local health club, I noticed several people reading magazines while strolling on the treadmill or cycling on the machines. But that level of intensity is not high enough to challenge and strengthen the body's systems to a new level of health. If you've been reading on the treadmill, put down the magazine and make the effort to work up a sweat. Once your endorphins (happy-making brain chemicals) kick in, you'll no longer be needing to entertain yourself with reading matter while you exercise—it'll be too much fun!

Ho'oponopono Prayer

Ho'oponopono is a Hawaiian prayer that was traditionally used by shamans to establish harmony with others and to clear any wrongs. It was about creating peace within communities. It was also practiced to release ourselves from belief systems that no longer served us.

I began using the prayer as a way to cleanse my personal struggles as well as clear the space when I engaged with others. I found by using this prayer, "I am sorry. Please forgive me. Thank you. I love you," that it felt like I was freeing myself of my past that was hindering new experiences. I wanted to be able to show up to my life as a clean slate. Now I know that's not possible to clear the slate, but I could certainly start new. It created a space where I felt new beginnings was possible. It created a space where I found forgiveness within myself and with others, the underlying life lesson of the heart.

I found myself practicing this prayer throughout my days. If a past story would arrive in my mind, I would say the prayer a dozen times. If I found myself in conflict with someone, I would come back to this prayer. I even began using it at random times—prior to a business call, driving in traffic, entering a new store, or before attending an event. Wherever I went, I found myself just reciting the prayer a handful of times in my mind. It not only put me in the present, but I felt connected to the Universe. I felt my soul. This simple practice has altered so many interactions and has brought about peace where I never thought possible.

Give it a try. The prayer is "I am sorry. Please forgive me. Thank you. I love you."

Heart Chakra Strategies for Balance

- Emphasize a plant-based dietary pattern.
- Eat bitter foods to nourish the heart.
- Incorporate sour and pungent flavors to remove stagnancy.
- Add omega-3 fatty acid foods through nuts, seeds, and cold-water fish.
- Eat green- and red-colored foods.
- Stay hydrated while eating high-fiber foods.
- Be mindful of damp foods, particularly excess sugar consumption.
- Sing and hum while you cook to deepen breath and reduce heart rate.
- Avoid eating late so not to interfere with liver's detoxification processes.
- Make the effort to share meals with others.

Self-Reflective Questions

The heart chakra embodies the theme of love. How open is your heart to life? Take the time to sit with these questions. You are at the tipping point in the chakra ladder of experiencing yourself more as an energetic being and less as a physical one. Let your emotions shine and explore what lessons in love are asking for your attention.

1. Are you experiencing any physical illnesses reflective of the heart chakra?
   a. Do you have heart disease?
   b. Do you have circulatory issues, indicated by cold hands/feet?
   c. Do you struggle with lung difficulties?
   d. Do you experience sinus infections/congestion/constipation?
   e. Have you had gallstones or your gallbladder removed?
2. Do you make your decisions with intellect, absent of emotional needs?

3. Do you have underlying anger or resentment?
4. Do you know what makes you happy? Are you open to asking and acting on the answers to that question?
5. Do you practice self-love?
6. Would you cook a full-course meal if intended only for yourself?
7. Do you have an aversion to bitter foods?
8. Do you tend to go for the sweets?
9. Do you avoid leafy greens and hearty vegetables if you can?
10. Do you find yourself frequently eating late at night?

CHAPTER 10

THROAT CHAKRA: SPEAK YOUR TRUTH

THROAT CHAKRA

Essence: Self-Expression
Life Lesson: Reclaiming Personal Authority
Physical: Throat/Neck/Mouth
Food: Sea Vegetables
Flavor: Pungent
Color: Blue

Arriving at the throat chakra, you have passed the tipping point on the chakra ladder, the heart chakra, and are moving further along the spectrum from physical to spiritual experience in life. The focus of the throat chakra, located at the base of the throat, is about making choices aligned with your truth.

The lower physical chakras—root, sacral, solar plexus—provide a foundation for you to be part of a family or community, interact personally with others, and develop how you relate to yourself. As your human experience becomes more heart-centered and you ascend the chakra ladder, you come into the throat chakra, where you focus on developing a resilient will and expressing yourself authentically.

Essential Nature: Self-Expression

The throat chakra is all about self-expression and communication: the choices you make and the truth you express. The Metal element, as discussed in stage 2, resonates with the throat chakra, signifying refinement to represent humans at their core, their essence or authenticity.

Self-expression takes different forms but always requires understanding yourself: what motivates your choices and where you engage your energy. You express yourself through speech, written word, and nonverbal forms as in gestures and body language. The stronger your energy flow to the throat, the more developed your communication skills, which include listening as well as speaking.

When balanced in the throat chakra, you have the courage to bring forth your true essence, to express your authentic self to the world. You are confident in decision-making, and you keep your word, not only to other people but also to yourself. Secure within yourself, you can separate your own thoughts and beliefs from those of others, ensuring your choices are aligned with your soul. Not only do you disengage from negative, external influences; you also refrain from imposing your personal standards on others. You have no judgments and no expectations.

When unbalanced, safety and control become immediate challenges. In attempting to find your grounding and inner strength, you may place strict rules and ideals on how life should be lived, try to micromanage others, and use your voice to dominate and control.

You know your throat chakra is unbalanced when you find yourself not following through on a commitment you made, making up excuses and stories about why. When consulting with clients, I have listened to many creative stories about why they couldn't stop drinking coffee, had no choice but to eat that third cookie, and how they unsuccessfully tried to drink more water. (How do you *try* to drink more water?)

Such excuses are a form of dishonesty, weakening the throat chakra energy and taking you further away for your truth. Think about where you have been less than honest with yourself or others. Perhaps you tell people what you think they want to hear to gain their acceptance. And why is it so difficult to make choices that you know are in your best interest? You want the change intellectually but fear making the choice emotionally. This is a sure sign the heart and mind are not aligned. The throat chakra is about bringing your soul's energy back to you, so you can own it and make choices from your most authentic self.

Life Lessons: Reclaiming Personal Authority

The life lessons of the throat chakra revolve around reclaiming your personal authority as connected to your higher power. Learning the lessons of this chakra requires you to start asking the question, Who or what has authority or power over me? The answer might be a belief, attitude, particular person, or a group you belong to.

A balanced throat chakra requires you to disengage from anything that holds a negative authority to hinder your personal evolution. Learn to bring awareness to those beliefs you hold, group attitudes you contribute to, or a particular person you're likely to run decisions by for approval and acceptance—and make some choices about them.

Each time you take back a piece of your soul's energy, you are connecting to and reclaiming your essence. You move further toward discovery of your authentic self and the wish to express your uniqueness to the world. When you sit aligned with your soul, heart, and mind harmonious, life is an adventure, fears evaporate, and you believe at the core of your being that everything is possible. Getting to this space is not an easy path, and many times the opportunity arrives in a crisis or crossroads, all coming back to you making a choice.

What you will discover is that releasing yourself from something or someone that you gave authority to is a sure way to start rocking the boat. With every shift, with every choice to take back your authority, you actually elevate your vibrational frequency to become more energy. Your life experiences start to dramatically change. The Universe responds when you say yes.

This isn't a clean, linear path. Expect to fall on and off course for a while, but make the choice to claim more ownership each time.

As your focus ascends the chakras, you lose sight of yourself as a solely physical being, surviving the mundane, day-to-day routines of life. You begin to realize that you are part of a bigger universal plan. Every choice you make has consequences, many of them happening on an energetic level where you may not witness their significance, yet know you are a contributor to the universal energy. Choices of integrity require personal authority and a surrendering to the divine—the lessons of the throat chakra.

Physiology of the Throat Chakra

The physiology of the throat chakra is focused on structures that further verbal communication: throat, trachea, larynx, and mouth, including jaw, teeth, and gums. The cervical vertebrae are also part of the throat chakra energies. Organs related to the throat chakra include lungs and thyroid gland.

The Metal element rules the throat chakra and resonates with the lungs and large intestine, two organs also associated with the sacral and heart chakras. Keep in mind that in a holistic model, you will experience the overlapping and interconnectivity of all aspects of who you are. This makes for a blending within the chakras, like a fluid dance, that strengthens their synergy.

The lungs, participating in an exchange with the external world, provide the air behind your voice so you can express your inner being to the outside world. Your ability to communicate resides here. The Metal element is about purification, so here you have the opportunity to choose what beliefs, attitudes, or situations no longer serve you and expel them. Here you speak your truth.

The large intestine is also linked to the sacral energies, another space of creativity, making it a reflection of your ability to let go and detach from what's draining energy away from you. The emotion of grief often comes up with any significant letting go. Even if the choice is in your best interest, there is still likely to be mourning of what once was. This is why spending time understanding self-love is so important. A healthy energy flow to the heart chakra from self-love will always influence whether you discover your essence and choose to show it to the world.

Physical Structures. When energy flow is unimpeded to the throat chakra, communication and creativity come easily to you. When the anatomy of speech is unobstructed, you speak with personal authority and confidence. There's an air of passion and inspiration in your tone. You speak up when warranted, operate from a space of honesty, and take full ownership of who you are.

When throat chakra energies are out of balance, you feel it physically, first in your voice. You may have a fear of speaking up or you talk excessively; you have a loud, domineering voice, or you are so soft-spoken that a whisper barely comes out. You may stutter or even stumble over your words. There can be a dominant, arrogant tone or one more passive-aggressive in nature. Observe how you or others communicate; there are so many messages conveyed just by a person's voice. Imbalances can also manifest as respiratory issues, laryngitis, sore throats, and tonsillitis along with gingivitis, periodontal disease, and jaw pain.

Organs. Regarding organs, the throat chakra is linked to the thyroid gland. The thyroid gland is part of the endocrine system that regulates metabolism. Metabolism is how your body breaks down food and converts it to energy for all your organs to use. The thyroid doesn't control metabolism on its own, but rather it takes direction from the pituitary gland and hypothalamus based on the amount of thyroid hormones circulating in the blood.

Many people struggle with thyroid disease, with a higher predominance being women. The thyroid may secrete too little hormone, as in Hashimoto's thyroiditis, or overproduce hormones, as in Graves' disease. It does appear that the root of these thyroid dysfunctions is autoimmune in nature.

Autoimmune conditions stem from systemic inflammation, a condition where the immune system ends up attacking its own tissues. When operating effectively, the immune system's role is to protect the body against foreign substances, as in bacteria or viruses. In cases of autoimmunity, the body does not recognize itself and responds by damaging the body's cells.

In Hashimoto's, antibodies slowly attack the thyroid cells resulting in low production of hormones necessary for metabolism. Symptoms many individuals struggle with include fatigue, constipation, dry skin, bouts of sadness, and weight gain that seems to occur without obvious reason prior to a diagnosis. Hashimoto's, the most common form of hypothyroidism, tends to lead to a low metabolic rate with weight gain happening more easily. This makes finding your personal dietary pattern a must. Otherwise the response to this weight gain is to try all the latest quick-fix diets, attempting to jump-start weight loss. In the end, these temporary fixes only alter metabolism even more.

In Graves' disease, the antibodies bind to receptors on the thyroid cells and stimulate them to release hormones in excess, causing an overactive thyroid. In these circumstances, you may feel symptoms of anxiety, shortness of breath, palpitations, changes in your menstrual cycle, and unexplained weight loss.

Ancient wisdom interprets dysfunction in the thyroid gland to be a block in energy flow with an emotional origin, specifically anger and sadness. There are links to the liver, lungs, and health of the stomach and spleen. This reinforces many connections between the chakras, with the root and solar plexus being intimately linked to the health of the throat chakra.

As we explore nutrition strategies in the next section, our discussion will cover strengthening immunity, along with potential dietary triggers that may be at the root of an autoimmune response.

Food and the Throat Chakra

Eating to nurture the throat chakra begins with addressing immunity, the first step being to align with the seasons as described in stage 2. Shifting food choices and even preparation techniques gives you more diversity in your dietary pattern, which is exactly what is needed to balance the throat chakra. The more foods you incorporate in your diet, the more potential immune-protective compounds and nutrients you introduce to your system. This is a great way to keep your digestion, home to your immunity, strong and adaptable.

This can be a challenge if decision-making is not your strong suit. One suggestion would be to begin exploring new cuisines and welcome taste profiles you have never experienced before. I have become a lover of Indian curries and Thai spice profiles. Be willing to explore!

Organic Foods. Immunity, tied to the digestive system and resonating with the essence of the Metal element, asks for you to eat what has been coined "clean," namely unprocessed foods from nature as close to their original state as possible. Choosing organic foods means your food supply will be free of pesticides, fungicides, antibiotics and hormones, ripening chemicals, food irradiation, and even genetically modified foods.

When someone with a compromised throat chakra and possible thyroid dysfunction has repeated exposures to chemically treated foods, it impacts their immune capabilities. This can lead to long-term immune suppression, disruption of hormones, and alteration of gene expression. Also, with each choice you make to eat clean, you join a larger movement that has the potential to shift how current farming conditions are performed, impacting the future food supply for generations to come.

The topic of genetically modified foods is controversial, with many scientists claiming that GMOs are safe to eat. But these altered foods haven't been around long enough for us to truly know the consequences of a lifetime of repeated exposure. What we do know is that when food is genetically engineered, its DNA is not found in nature; the chemical and energetic signature of the food has been altered.

The immune system is more than a first line of defense against foreign invaders. It is an electromagnetic sensory system that interprets and communicates at the molecular level. Back in the late 1990s when GMOs became abundant on the grocery shelves, there were studies showing correlations to altered intestinal permeability and chronic inflammatory processes.

This will continue to be a debate because the reality of the nutritional studies is that research supports both sides of the argument. Current nutritional studies come with many layers of interpretation and validity because of the difficulty to reduce overall health to only one factor. You are a multisensory being with such complexity that linear, reductionist approaches don't even come close to representing all of who you are.

The questions to ask is, What works for me? Once again, your choice is so much bigger than what you throw into the grocery cart each week. You are choosing foods created by nature, closest to their original state, which we know without debate makes a difference.

As I've said repeatedly, one of the best things you can do for immunity is to eat a rainbow diet. Every color resonates with a chakra, and the throat chakra energies, being the home of choice, has an active partnership with each color. The deeper the colors, the better. Look down at your plate and see a colorful masterpiece. Immunity is about having a strong foundation yet being flexible and adaptable to whatever environments you may encounter, inside or out.

A simple, practical way to eat a rainbow diet is to make soups a part of daily eating. Soups fuse the chakra foods together in a perfect liquid medium for proper digestion, providing a powerhouse of nutrients. Soups are the most nourishing foods you can eat. Check out the health-supportive soup recipes I share in the appendix of this book.

A client's first response often is "What? Eat soup in the summer? It's too hot out!" That may be true, but warm weather doesn't stop people from eating cooked food in the summer. Cheeseburgers, pizza, and grilled chicken are staples in many American summertime diets. These foods not only are hot in temperature but have a warming thermal nature. Instead, eat vegetables, grains, and legumes with an innate cooling nature during hot times. Some cooling foods are celery, mushrooms, chard, watercress, millet, and mung and navy beans.

I love soup! There's nothing better than starting the day with a bowl of traditional miso soup. Miso is a fermented soybean paste that originated in China thousands of years ago. Being a fermented food, containing live bacteria, it aids in digestion and assimilation of food along with a growing list of antioxidants that are being identified. With its sweet-salty flavor, it becomes a great supporter of the throat chakra's need to combat dryness, leaving a moistening effect necessary for clear speech and self-expression.

Miso soup also commonly contains leafy greens, scallions, mushrooms, and seaweed. Mushrooms have been used medicinally in Eastern medicine and are known in modern science for their antiviral and immune-enhancing properties. Seaweeds are also nutrient dense with detoxifying, alkalizing, and digestive health benefits. Miso soup is the perfect blend of nutrients and energetic essence unifying your entire energy field in one bowl. Consider adding into your dietary pattern using a food rotation approach. Remember: keep diversity in your life!

Gluten and Casein Allergens. In general, food allergies are a part of our overall immunity and inflammatory processes. With the thyroid gland being tied to the throat energies and the potential of autoimmune problems, maintaining a strong immune system along with removing specific food allergens warrants a discussion here.

There is a strong link between certain dietary proteins and autoimmune diseases. The two main protein allergens are gliadin (a protein from the gluten in some grains, such as wheat and rye) and casein (protein found in cow's milk). An autoimmune response comes from a combination of exposure to one of these proteins in a person with a compromised digestive system and impaired immunity.

When wheat or dairy are a frequent part of your diet, a low-grade inflammatory response with specific thyroid antibodies can occur. Over time, thyroid function is compromised, altering the metabolic processes throughout your body. The correlation is not always obvious because it doesn't cause an allergic reaction that has you going into anaphylactic shock. Rather, it's one in which you may start to see dark circles under your eyes, suffer from indigestion and constipation, experience alterations in cognitive function or mood, and have overall feelings of fatigue.

Food marketing has programmed us to eat whole grains, with the term *whole wheat* becoming synonymous with a healthy choice. This is not to say wheat is unhealthy. With the growing demand and marketing influences, most wheat is a highly processed food (unless you are purchasing the whole kernel as in organic, wheat berries, or faro) and for the most part a genetically modified product. Furthermore, you can find gluten in canned soups, salad dressings, and lunch meats as *hydrolyzed vegetable protein*, *modified food starch*, and *maltodextrin* appearing on ingredient labels.

In addition, we were brought up being told, "Drink your milk; it makes you strong." Do you remember the famous celebrity milk mustache commercials? There is major controversy with these health claims. First, cow's milk has a much different protein composition and quantity than human breast milk. Both have the main purpose of feeding offspring in the early stages of life, but cow's milk can be quite difficult for many humans to digest and assimilate.

The blame for milk allergy has been put on the sugar lactose for so long; however, the protein casein triggers damage to the intestinal lining and in Eastern approaches is said to produce dampness and phlegm. Dampness leads to qi stagnation and blockages of the free flow of energy through the body. Over time, blocked energy meridians create inflammation. Damp illnesses include bronchitis, asthma, allergies, coronary heart disease, chronic fatigue, sinusitis, arthritis, and a dysfunctional digestive system.

Keep in mind that autoimmune diseases can create a direct response to a particular organ or gland; however, at the root, it is a systemic inflammatory issue. This makes strengthening your immunity and digestive health imperative to addressing thyroid conditions.

Pungent Flavor. A pungent flavor stimulates the lungs, bringing energy up and outward. It helps in removing stagnation and opening energy flow, providing an active yang energy in support of self-expression and communication. Pungent flavors can have warming or cooling thermal effects on the body, so consider your personal needs and the outside weather when choosing. Warming pungent foods include garlic, onion, fennel, ginger, basil, and scallions. Cooling pungent foods include peppermint, radishes, watercress, and cabbage.

Blue-Colored Foods. The color blue resonates with the throat chakra along with the complementary color of orange that matches the other creativity energy center, the sacral chakra. Blue foods do not necessarily exist, so orange foods are more emphasized. Orange foods as in squash, carrots, tangerines, mangos, and peaches can be quite helpful to nurture and balance the throat chakra.

Strategies for Balance

Eating with balancing the throat chakra in mind requires awareness of your eating behaviors and individual needs. When you take the time to observe your food choices, there is an opportunity to understand yourself better.

For many, shifting their relationship with food feels like a form of punishment, as if something is being taken away from them. I have yet to meet someone who declares with excitement, "I'm on a diet!" as they walk into work Monday morning with their Ziploc of mini carrots and a priceless expression of misery. There's a huge difference in the mindset of restricting food choices for going on a diet and positively shifting your relationship with food.

We have all met or have been that classic dieter. You name it, you've tried it. It was always about what we had to give up, like sweets or fried foods, that we became so preoccupied with the offensive food that we finally caved and ate it. On to the next unsuccessful diet we went. That cycle won't change until you see that it is not about depriving yourself of something but instead about adding options and creating more meal choices.

Variety in the diet is a big part of my recommended food strategies for the throat chakra energies. Expand your palate! With each new food you are willing to experience, you increase options within your dietary pattern and your menu of possibilities is expanding. You may prefer certain foods; however, consuming a more diverse spectrum of foods not only increases nutritional benefits and keeps digestion strong and adaptable but can even enhance your self-expression and authentic communication.

Awareness Exercise

How aware are you of how you invest and engage your soul's energy?

For an entire day, or even a week, consciously watch yourself while you interact with others. Bring awareness to your tone of voice along with the level of confidence behind your words.

Is there any passion behind your communication? Do you change the details of stories, agree with others so not to cause conflict, or make excuses for why you haven't completed things? What's happening in your thoughts? What stories from your past are you telling—or future ones are you creating—in your mind that is keeping you from being present?

Watch where your energy is going. Can you make a conscious choice to bring your soul's energy back and claim personal authority for your communications?

Throat Chakra Strategies for Balance

- Keep your dietary pattern clean or unprocessed with immune-supportive foods.
- Incorporate soups into your daily regimen, connecting all your chakras.
- Eat pungent foods to nourish the lungs.
- Consume moistening foods to manage dryness.
- Include sea vegetables and iodine-rich foods.
- Have most of your meals cooked, limiting raw foods.
- Stay hydrated while eating high-fiber root vegetables.

- Consider removing gluten and dairy from your diet.
- Bring awareness to your eating behaviors.
- Diversify your palate.

Self-Reflective Questions

With increased self-awareness and self-knowledge, you can begin to make decisions from the seat of your will. It's time to be honest with yourself and ask the tough questions of where you give away your personal power and why. Denying, dodging, or overcompensating only results in rigid, judgmental, and perfectionist ways of living. This blocks you from expressing your authentic self to the world.

Sit with these questions for as long as you need, revisiting them over time. Remember this is a journey not an end point to achieve.

1. Are you experiencing any physical illnesses reflective of the throat chakra?
   a. Respiratory issues (asthma, chronic cough, shortness of breath)?
   b. Do you have thyroid issues (hypo- or hyperthyroidism)?
   c. Do you have other autoimmune diseases (type 1 diabetes or celiac)?
   d. Do you have gum or teeth problems (gingivitis, periodontal disease, teeth erosion)?
   e. Do you grind your teeth and have TMJ pain?
   f. Do you get frequent bouts of laryngitis?
   g. Do you get frequent sore throats or swollen glands?
   h. Do you have troubles with your cervical spine (stenosis, herniation, scoliosis)?
   i. Do you have a compromised immunity? Get colds and infections frequently?
   j. Are you internally dry, including dry skin?
2. How many diets have you been on and quit?

3. Have you accepted that changing your relationship with food will require changes in all other areas of your life, that every choice has rippling consequences?

4. Why do you give yourself a pass to back out of a commitment, starting with your food changes?

5. Who or what has control over your will?

6. Can you operate from a space of honesty?

7. Are you waiting for a safe move in order to make a decision?

8. Are you indecisive, either relying on someone else to make decision or finding yourself waiting until the last minute to react?

9. Do you carry a belief that you are trapped or restricted when you shift your food choices?

10. Do you have known food sensitivities to gluten or dairy?

CHAPTER 11

THE THIRD EYE CHAKRA: OPEN YOUR INNER SIGHT

THIRD EYE CHAKRA

Essence: Inner Vision
Life Lesson: Detachment
Physical: Brain/Autonomic Nervous System
Food: Fats and Sugars
Flavor: Sweet
Color: Indigo

After reclaiming your will at the throat chakra level of consciousness and energy, you arrive at the third eye chakra, located in the center of the forehead. Here the focus is about accessing your inner vision, going beyond reasoning to tap into guidance from the universal source within. Such insight allows you to peel back the layers of who you are and move beyond present-day paradigms.

Essential Nature: Inner Vision

The third eye chakra is about inner vision. No longer looking out to the external world for guidance, you begin to look within for your source of identity. This is the time when masks come off, vulnerabilities are exposed, and you are left to explore the illusions you've constructed to help you feel secure in life.

Life Lessons: Detachment

Detachment is the lesson of the third eye chakra, meaning the ability to step back from a situation and take an impersonal view of events. When a crisis or major change presents itself in your life, it means time for change—the direction of your life is being shifted. You can choose how you respond to such events, either as a victim or as someone being offered an opportunity to see past the five senses.

It's amazing how attached we can become to playing victim. I've played the role way too well. I'm talking Oscar worthy. It's such an easy mentality to slip into, especially when we are living in survival mode and only see life through our five senses. It has been difficult, at times painful, with expanding moments of freedom, choosing to stand in that space knowing I was not merely a bystander in any of my life events. I played a part. It all came down to the art of detachment.

Detachment does not mean that you do not care; rather, it means you are willing to look beyond the superficial layer of what is happening and see the people and circumstances as teachers bringing you to another level of liberated consciousness.

As you begin experiencing the lessons of the third eye, know that the ability to go within, face fears, and create a new reality is all about *you*, not those around you. Don't expect others to jump at the thought of living consciously, let alone be inspired by your newfound principles of life. Each person is at his or her particular point on the path of personal evolution. This means many of your old relationships, groups, and environments may no longer work for you.

This may mean spending less time with friends who are not on this journey. Perhaps you sign up for the cycling group at the local gym, join at outdoor adventure club, or begin taking recreational cooking classes to meet new friends. Although there will be times of fear and pain, do your best to look for the bigger picture.

Through your thoughts and experiences, you create your reality. You see what you want to see. Conscious living is what is going to begin the process to distinguish the difference between illusion and truth. Each time you take the cosmic perspective, moving toward inner knowing, your responses to life's circumstances evolve along with your compassion for others. You eventually reach the understanding that you are simultaneously a physical and energetic being, part of grander universal plan that extends past what you can see with your limited five senses.

Physiology of the Third Eye Chakra

The third eye chakra is connected to the eyes, pineal gland, autonomic nervous system, and brain.

Eyes. Our eyes are connected through the optic tract to the higher parts of our brains. The brain's frontal lobe—the place of reason, memory, and decision-making—is where our free will resides. Conscious choice resides at this level, and so you have the capacity to choose what you place your attention on, both inside and outside yourself.

Clearly visualizing your goals, whether through daydreaming or intentionally creating a vision board, inspires you to act and move forward, showing you what is soon to become physically manifested in your life. For me, a visualization meditation as my future self has been incredibly powerful.

If you see the world through a lens of gratitude, you will find life full of endless things to be grateful for. If you see the world as a place that always rejects you, as I once did, you will encounter situations that bring rejection into your life. Struggles with sight, including blurred vision, cataracts, glaucoma, nearsightedness or farsightedness, tunnel vision, and ocular hypertension originate within the third eye chakra, all related to an unwillingness to see life through the lens of personal truth.

Pineal Gland. The pineal gland, known for centuries as the third eye, is closely linked to the hypothalamus and pituitary glands, which are the master glands of the body's hormonal processes. The pineal gland is said to be the place where intuition resides. Through exposure to light, your hypothalamus transmits a message to the pineal gland through the sympathetic nervous system. The pineal gland then releases the hormone melatonin, controlling your biological circadian rhythm along with the regulation of reproductive hormones.

You have a circadian rhythm in which physical, mental, and behavioral changes occur through a twenty-four-hour cycle and are influenced by internal factors as well as environmental signals, especially light. Natural sunlight stimulates the optic nerve, sending signals to the brain via the hypothalamus to regulate and balance your internal processes.

With the regulation of waking and sleep patterns determined by this glandular function, many find themselves struggling with nights of insomnia and may even become trapped in a recurring nightmare for months. Dreams link us to the unconscious mind, and if insightfully explored, can help us to see something in our waking time in a different light.

Autonomic Nervous System. The third eye chakra is energetically linked to the autonomic nervous system (ANS). The ANS is where involuntary actions occur, such as digestion, cell growth and renewal, blood filtering, and regulation of heart rate and blood pressure. The ANS takes little effort on your part, for the most part working beyond your conscious awareness. However, when you travel through life on autopilot, you lose a conscious connection with your body, and these vital functions become compromised and decline in efficiency. It's then time to bring these functions into your conscious awareness.

Brain. Scientists have a greater understanding of the brain's workings than ever before. With the advancements in technology, the living brain and its continuous plasticity can be observed. You and I, as children growing up, were taught in school that there were only a certain number of brain cells, and the functions of our brains were fixed and would not grow as we aged.

But today, that is not the case. We now know that the brain can generate new brain cells through our entire lifespan by a process called neurogenesis. Even better, you can continue to learn and develop new synaptic connections that literally rewire your circuits through a process called neuroplasticity. How incredible is that? Just as your genes can become altered in their expression, so can your brain cells!

The brain houses the mind, and your mind is incredibly powerful in its capacity to transform your health. For every thought you have, you produce chemicals in the brain that travel down to your body, so you can feel what you are thinking. The constant thoughts running through your mind, which are estimated to be the same 90 percent as yesterday, are what create your state of being. Your thoughts (mind) and your physiology (body) are continually working together to alter your health, whether in a positive or challenging way.

Dr. Joe Dispenza, first in his book, *Evolve Your Brain*, and more recently in *You Are the Placebo*, explored this process of how thoughts literally become matter. He even went a step further to state that if you can change your thoughts, you can change your physiology and thus transform your health.

Intellect resides in the third eye chakra along with imagination, visualization, and insight. I can be considered a left-brain thinker, rational with a nice dose of overanalyzing. For so long, I followed the rules! If there weren't any rules, I would create them. I was convinced I could use my brain to fix any situation, but always to the exclusion of using my emotions.

At the end of the day, in order for life to shift and expand, heart and mind need to be aligned. This is a challenging feat because we seek safety, consistency, and the familiar, even if we know behind the mask it's not the best choice. Many, like myself, were raised to operate from intellect but without emotions, seeing the exploration of emotions as a sign of weakness.

But emotions are important. Did you know you can become chemically addicted to feeling a certain way? Feelings of sadness, anxiety, or shame all flood an array of chemicals through your body to support your thoughts. When you choose differently, it physically doesn't feel right because you are creating a new, unfamiliar inner environment. That's when most people put their masks back on and run for the hills of safety.

However, if you keep wearing masks for safety, you eventually become your genetics. "You're just like your father/mother!" is a comment that makes most of us cringe. But if you are not willing to go within, explore your vulnerabilities and shadow behaviors, you will be living the neurological platform you inherited.

It takes getting away from the belief "That's me—I've always been that way." We are actually choosing to be that way by not looking deeper within. We have the capacity to rewire, create new synaptic connections, and reinvent ourselves. It is not an overnight process, and it does ask you to take ownership of who you are. But it will completely change your life. For every door that closes, it is imperative that you remain present, with an insightful eye. Another door is always opening—it's just up to you to see it.

If you choose to contemplate your life and get out of your familiar box, you will forever be changed. Your energetic field will shift, your vibration will elevate, and you will see life through a different lens. Your relationship with food, and consequently your health, cannot change if you remain the same person energetically. As Einstein stated, "Problems cannot be solved with the same mindset that created them." When you shift your openness to life, becoming more receptive to the world and creating a space to dream, life's possibilities grow exponentially. Your evolution will not go unnoticed. People will see and feel it in your presence. Once again, for every choice you make toward your authentic self, you are inspiring others to do the same.

Food for the Third Eye Chakra

Supportive eating for the third eye chakra begins with nourishing the brain through healthy fats and carbohydrates. Having a healthy brain is essential to having a healthy mind. When brain functions are compromised, cognitive function decline shows up in memory, decision-making, concentration, and mood.

As mentioned earlier, the heart and brain (mind) are aligned, physiologically and energetically. This means that whatever impacts your heart also impacts your brain. If you are struggling with the emotional energies of the heart chakra or have already manifested physical symptoms such as inflammation or hypertension, it is going to have a direct effect on your brain. You can easily see diminished abilities in memory, concentration, and mood. The result is a shift away from the higher brain centers, stopping evolution and making you become more animalistic in your nature. You may find yourself more stubborn and set in your ways, possibly prone to agitation and even depression and aggression.

Again, such a scenario demonstrates the holistic paradigm of interconnectivity in which everything is connected to everything else.

Keeping this in mind, finding self-love in the heart chakra will influence the incidence of stroke and Alzheimer's disease in the brain. The brain-heart connection also calls for some nourishing eating strategies, similar to the needs of the heart, starting with the consumption of fats.

Fats. The brain is 60 percent fat, making it the fattiest organ in the body, and the types of fats you consume change the shape and function of your brain cells. Fats are molded into the physical structure of the cell membranes and myelin sheath coverings of brain cells, impacting their ability to function. Some fats such as omega-3 fatty acids enhance cognitive function, while others like trans-fatty acids diminish intellect.

It's not only types of fats that can alter your brain; it's also the ratio of each kind of fat in your diet. Omega-3 fatty acids (DHA) make up about half the fat in brain cells, making them essential to nourish the brain. Having a high DHA content makes the cell membranes more fluid, adding flexibility and making communication between brain cells more efficient. Cognitive function is not exclusive to the number of brain cells you have; it's more about their ability to form neural connections with other cells and communicate. When a cell membrane is more fluid, it has a higher amount of responsive insulin receptors, insulin being a hormone essential to feeding the brain.

Insulin is the hormone that is responsible for the uptake of glucose (sugar) into the cells, and glucose is the brain's preferred fuel source. The brain is in constant need of glucose to fulfill the high energy demands of its functioning. Through recent research findings, we've learned that insulin plays a role in the brain beyond glucose metabolism to the formation of new neural networks, giving you the ability to concentrate, learn, and remember. In addition to its role in neuron communication, DHA reduces inflammatory activity while influencing concentrations of neurotransmitters, such as serotonin, acetylcholine, and dopamine.

A low intake of DHA-rich foods in your dietary pattern increases the possibility of depression, Alzheimer's, and Parkinson's disease. Incorporating fish into your diet is a great way to maintain flexibility in your brain cells and therefore the function of your mind. Consider adding fish rich in omega-3 fatty acids, such as wild salmon, halibut, yellowfin tuna, sardines, and anchovies to your menu. If you choose not to eat any animal-based foods, the body can convert the fats found in green, leafy vegetables, walnuts, almonds, pumpkin seeds, soybeans, hemp seeds, and seaweed into beneficial omega-3 fatty acids.

The important message here is that it is the ratio of the different types of fats that is a major determining factor in brain function. Excess consumption of saturated fats is going to do the opposite of what polyunsaturated omega-3 fatty acids do, making cell membranes more rigid and less flexible. The more saturated fats you eat, the more tightly packed the membrane's structure becomes, making it difficult for nutrients to pass through while reducing the receptor's ability to configure and mold to neurotransmitters that are trying to communicate with the cell.

Be careful not to jump into black-and-white thinking around fats and oils. A raw, unheated coconut oil along with some organic clarified butter, both structurally saturated, can have medicinal and health promoting effects on the body. Understand you still need some saturated fat in your diet for optimal brain cell functioning. Just ease up on the animal foods, Alfredo sauces, and high-fat cheeses. It's more about your long-term patterns of eating meat, along with the addition of processed fats, hydrogenated and trans in nature. Those fats are found in packaged or premade foods such as bakery goods, margarine, microwave popcorn, and anything fried. These are all associated with diminished memory and learning, depression, hostility, and a higher prevalence of stroke and dementia.

A brain-boosting dietary pattern is one that supports a plant-based diet. Animal foods come with a high price tag of pro-inflammatory properties, causing effects not conducive to a healthy mind.

Carbohydrates. Since glucose (sugar) is the brain's main source of fuel, the consumption of carbohydrates comes into play when considering brain health. Plants closest to their original state are some of the best sources of carbohydrates to feed your brain, especially legumes; whole (not milled) grains; and high-fiber, hearty vegetables.

The brain can only store a minuscule amount of glucose, needing a steady supply coming in for it to function. Managing glucose levels through foods that allow for slower glucose absorption is most beneficial. Some highly suggested foods would be adzuki beans, mung beans, tempeh, quinoa, steel-cut oats, cauliflower, broccoli, and brussels sprouts.

Be mindful of your consumption of high concentrated sugar foods. Chronic high blood sugar levels not only lead to the development of diabetes but can degrade your memory while increasing the probability of dementia. Watch out for the caffeinated, sugary drinks touted to improve your concentration, elevate your metabolism, and burn off fat. We may want to buy these types of drinks to combat the drowsy effects of insomnia, but in the end, they diminish awareness and cognitive function.

Stimulants, for example caffeine, block brain receptors so that neurotransmitters dopamine and adrenaline will surge, making you feel motivated and alert. The problem is frequent use alters the natural production of these brain chemicals, making you become addicted to your caffeinated sugar drink or cup of coffee. The expression on a client's face when I suggest they stop drinking coffee for a period of time never gets old.

These adrenaline-boosting stimulants are also vasoconstrictors, decreasing blood flow to the brain, interfering with sleep, and dehydrating your tissues. Hydration is essential to brain function, with 90 percent of your blood being water. That's how oxygen and nutrients get where they need to be. Consider shifting away from the sugars and stimulants and consuming more water. That way, your brain can relearn how to function on its own natural brain motivators.

Sweet Flavor. The flavors most resonant with the third eye energies are sweet and pungent. Whole grains and beans provide sweetness, especially when thoroughly chewed. This will give grounding to the root while you go within to explore deeper layers of who you are. A pungent flavor stimulates movement and helps you shake off stagnancy. The third eye is about removing illusions, old patterns of thought, and moving into a new space where you peel away masks to discover your authentic self. Consider adding cumin, curry, cardamom, ginger, basil, pepper, turmeric, and mustard to your cooking.

Purple and Yellow Foods. The color of the third eye chakra is indigo, making purple foods, as well as the complementary color yellow of the solar plexus chakra, an additional support for drawing down energy flow to nourish and heal at this level of consciousness. Purple foods, carrying the vibrational frequency of the third eye, also contains strong antioxidant power in their phytonutrient anthocyanidins.

Consider adding purple grapes, blueberries, blackberries, pluots, figs, and raisins to your dietary pattern. Also add some yellow foods, such as lemons, pineapple, pears, squash, and yellow carrots. A balanced solar plexus chakra, home of your self-esteem and inner courage, is essential for you to be willing to go within and explore your fears.

Strategies for Balance

The third eye chakra is about being open to seeing your relationship with food in a different light. What beliefs about food that are not based in truth do you hide behind? Going beyond the five senses, here you experience intuitive eating. Pay attention to how your body feels and what foods you gravitate toward. Become insightful as to how these foods impact your energetic being. I understand how the illusion of staying in the intellect for safety works, but this is going to make it difficult, almost impossible, for a true shift in your relationship with food—and life, for that matter.

When you get in your head, the overanalyzing begins, and you start counting calories, measuring grams of carbohydrates, and obsessing about the numbers on the scale. It's easy to take nutrition to an extreme, trying to use our intellect to control everything. We may find ourselves weighing in on the scale daily while reducing the meaning of food to its caloric intake, regardless of its quality.

When it comes to recipes, do your best not to take them so literally. Recipes are guidelines, so let your creativity flow. I promise you won't get in trouble for changing the ingredients or technique. Can you loosen your restrictions and rules around food? Can you find a more flexible nature and start to see food differently? Reductionist thinking will never allow for the cosmic perspective. I can share that when you do begin living more intuitively, you will laugh about how many years or decades you spent looking at food solely through the lens of calories and composition.

Making choices to eat and live more intuitively and with insight means that life as you know it is going to change. You are physically rewiring your brain and elevating your energetic vibration with the outcome of a more expansive life. This may entail shifting the company you keep, how you socialize, even where you live or work. Changing how you perceive food is an initiator of change in your life.

Create a Vision and Meditate

Your thoughts and visions are the beginning of what manifests in your physical life. Creating a vision board is one way to feel inspired and bring your dreams, creative endeavors, and general life wishes into form.

Here's how: Using any board, from a corkboard to even the screen of your computer, start collecting photos, images, and quotes that inspire you regarding what you wish to become and experience. The key is to take time each day and visualize these dreams and circumstances as if they have already happened.

The most effective way to get into our subconscious programming, where real change happens, is through meditation. Begin with a mindful meditation where you place your attention on your breath. Just watch it. Do not try to control the inhale and exhale; just observe. If a thought wanders in, which it will, just bring your attention back to your breath. The intention here is to be mindful. Observe the thought and go back to your breath. Over time, the moments in between thoughts will extend, helping you become present for longer periods of time. After being in this mindful meditation for a minimum of ten minutes, begin to visualize a day in your new life. What would a day in that life look like? What would you do? Who would you share it with? And most importantly, how would you feel? Place yourself in the feeling of your new reality, of what you wish to create. In order to receive, become grateful before it arrives.

The key to successful visualization practices is to experience gratitude before what you want to happen has actually happened. Let your emotions flow. You need to *feel* it! Heart and mind aligned—that's when the Universe conspires to make things happen. Then take action, no matter how big or small, in the direction of what you seek.

Third Eye Chakra Strategies for Balance

- Emphasize a plant-based dietary pattern.
- Add omega-3 fatty acid foods through nuts, seeds, and cold-water fish.
- Minimize saturated and hydrogenated oils in your diet.
- Take in the sweet flavor through whole grains, legumes, and vegetables.
- Add pungent spices to your cooking to remove stagnancy.
- Incorporate fermented foods for maintaining digestive health.
- Eat purple and yellow foods.
- Be aware of excess caffeine and stimulant use.
- Allow your intuition to be a part of your food choices.
- Avoid reducing food to calories and grams of protein.

Self-Reflective Questions

The third eye chakra challenges you to see food differently. It asks for you to peel away the illusions you may have about your relationship with food, gain some insight, and know you can rewire neural circuits, alter the expression of your genes, and elevate your energetic vibration. All of these possibilities begin with awareness. Take the time to reflect on the questions below.

1. Are you experiencing any physical illnesses reflective of the third eye chakra?
   a. Are you experiencing vision problems (cataracts, glaucoma, farsightedness/nearsightedness, ocular hypertension)?
   b. Do you struggle with headaches or migraines?
   c. Do you have insomnia, trouble sleeping, or staying asleep?
2. Are you willing to look within and explore your fears and vulnerabilities?
3. Do you believe you are part of larger universal plan?

4. Can you visualize what you wish for and feel it as if it has come true?
5. Are you afraid of the changes in your life if you were to live healthier and change your relationship with food?
6. Do you eat intuitively, or is it more an intellectual experience?
7. Are you mindful of how you feel with your current food choices? Especially your favorite ones?
8. Do you consider yourself addicted to caffeine or other stimulants?
9. Are you hanging on to an old relationship with food?
10. Do you find you overanalyze situations?

CHAPTER 12

CROWN CHAKRA: CONNECT TO THE DIVINE

CROWN CHAKRA

Essence: Higher Self/Spirituality
Life Lesson: Living in Present Moment
Physical: Central Nervous System
Food: Fasting
Flavor: All
Color: Purple/White

We have arrived at the crown chakra, the highest vibration energy vortex in the chakra system, linking you directly to the Universe. Located at the top of the head, the crown is the point at which the life force enters your body and travels down through the descending chakras, bringing spirit into physical reality. As the root connects you to the Earth and everything physical, the crown connects you to the divine, your Highest Self.

Essential Nature: Higher Self / Spirituality

Traveling up the chakras in consciousness, you arrive at a liberated and expanded way of living. The crown chakra is about finding connection to everything—both within yourself and ultimately to the Universe. When the crown is balanced, you operate simultaneously from all aspects of who you are—body, mind, and soul. You do not deny, ignore, or disconnect from any part of yourself. You look at life through a cosmic lens, grasping the holistic paradigm and grander picture of all life's events. You have met your soul.

When energies of the crown chakra are balanced, you are inspired, welcome new ideas, and feel a level of faith in the Universe's larger plan. You are able to remain in the present, placing your attention on what is right in front of you, the key to changing your neural networks and navigating through life differently.

If crown chakra energies are blocked, you find yourself fixed in your beliefs, overthinking and overanalyzing life. Climbing through the chakras and elevating your vibrational energy requires you to release any attachment you have to beliefs or even things in the material world and trust the Universe's orchestration of a much larger dynamic than the everyday world you may see.

Have you ever been in a conversation with someone and were able to step outside yourself to watch yourself having the conversation? That observer is your silent witness, the presence that is always there behind whatever is happening. Such an awareness of your soul can shift your entire outlook on life. You feel a genuine openness to new experiences, a level of calmness within, and a sense of faith like you've never felt before.

The crown chakra brings up the world of spirituality and a faith in the unfolding of your life. You function from a space of curiosity and seek full experiences, emotions included. The right side of the brain, the creative and intuitive side, takes on a larger presence in your life.

For many of my clients, the concept of spirituality and connecting with their soul was woo-woo and for the psychic people. Most did not consider themselves holy rollers but did celebrate religious holidays. Where religion plays a role in the group mind of the root chakra, spirituality is about your individual relationship to the Universe. This connection is the essence of the crown chakra.

Experiencing life through a cosmic lens requires being in the present moment. This makes it possible not only to notice coincidences or synchronicities in life but to act upon them.

Life Lesson: Living in the Present Moment

Living in the present moment is the lesson of the crown chakra, and the present is where your life changes. Showing up completely in each moment of your life has you seeing with clarity. How often have you been distracted by keeping stories of your past alive in your daily thoughts, always so worried about what might be happening next that you miss what is right in front of you?

Cooking in the kitchen can became a valuable form of meditation. Meditation, along with prayer, is a way to connect to your soul and the divine. Through meditation, you can remove distractions and learn how to have a focused attention—to be present. That's the first step in observing what is going on within you. Many times when the topic of meditation arises, an image of the Buddha sitting under a tree follows. Buddhism teaches a form of meditation, but that may not work for everyone, especially those who are completely new to any kind of self-inquiry. It is possible to bring the art of meditation into the modern world. This is where your relationship with food can help.

Consider using your time cooking in the kitchen as a form of meditation. Cooking is an opportunity to be mindful, placing your attention on one task and clearing your mind of incessant chatter. As a first "cooking to be present" activity, I suggest a winter vegetable stew, a task that requires a good amount of peeling, chopping, and dicing of vegetables. At first, you may meet the task with resistance, completely flabbergasted by how many vegetables could possibly go into one pot. What you will find is that the repetitive acts of food preparation can have a calming effect. Allow your kitchen to provide you with a space for relaxation and destressing and serve as a learning environment. The kitchen can be your first place to begin challenging fixed beliefs about what constitutes the best choices for your health.

Physiology of the Crown Chakra

The crown chakra is a continuation of the third eye chakra, and both are intimately linked to the workings of the brain. Recall that the third eye chakra connects to the autonomic nervous system, or innate intelligence that makes all the involuntary actions in the body happen beyond our conscious awareness. The crown chakra adds another layer of complexity through the central nervous system with a blend of intellect and intuition still present. Other areas linked to the crown chakra are the endocrine system (pituitary gland and hypothalamus glands) and the skin.

Physical manifestations of compromised energy flow to the crown chakra include migraines, neurological disorders, brain tumors, multiple personality disorders, insomnia, skin conditions, and learning disabilities.

Central Nervous System. The CNS consists of the brain and spinal cord, making it the control center for the body. Both the brain and spinal cord coordinate in carrying out their functions. The brain interprets all sensory information with the goal of maintaining balance within the body, a process termed homeostasis. The spinal cord carries signals back and forth from the brain to the peripheral nerves, so the brain and muscles can communicate. One part of the brain is the cerebellum. Along with aspects of language, memory, and learning, the cerebellum controls motor movements that include coordination and balance. This is the part of the brain that helps you perform physical movements.

Experiences with our physical balance are tied to the crown chakra energies. Many like to blame slowed-down reflexes on getting older, but you don't have to play the age card until you hit your late eighties. Your chronological age does not correlate with health as much as your biological and psychological age does. Chronological age is only a number that goes with the yearly calendar.

What does your chronological age really do for you? It gets you booze and discounts. That's it. Biological age demonstrates how your internal environment responds to how you live. Each organ, tissue, and individual cell responds in its own way to your life choices. It is not a linear or predictable pattern. Psychological age is how old you feel, experienced all the way down to the cellular level. So if you woke up today feeling like you were twenty again (if that was a good year for you), that's what your cells are going to respond to. If you woke with thoughts of being old, whatever age you believe that to be, that's what you are communicating to your cells. Your lifestyle choices of nutrition, exercise, conditioned beliefs, and daily thoughts running through your mind are continuously impacting your health. (To read more about this, I refer you to *Ageless Body, Timeless Mind* by Deepak Chopra.)

Pituitary and Hypothalamus Glands. The CNS and the endocrine system work together in a holistic operation to coordinate all the body's systems. The nervous system sends signals through nerve impulses while the endocrine system releases hormones to impact body's activities. The difference is nerve impulses happen instantaneously while the secretion of hormones can take a longer time for the body to respond to, from minutes to hours to even days. Both systems are enmeshed with the principal goal of maintaining a balanced inner environment.

This brings the glands of the crown chakra energies, the pituitary and hypothalamus glands, into the conversation. The pituitary gland works closely with the hypothalamus to stimulate or inhibit the production of hormones from other endocrine glands. Their interaction impacts the physiological processes of all cells, including thyroid, kidney, and reproductive, connecting these endocrine glands intimately to the CNS.

Skin. Your skin, the largest organ in the body, is linked to the crown chakra energies. In traditional Chinese medicine, the skin is referred to as your "third lung" because of its ability to breathe. Through the skin's pores, nutrients are absorbed while toxins are excreted through perspiration. The skin is highly sensitive, secreting hormones that make it much more than a protective barrier, but also a way to communicate you to the world. Recall that every cell is designed to regenerate to a state of newness, so that you are physically a new person within each decade of your life. Your skin renews itself almost every month and is a physical reflection of your inner thoughts and feelings.

In times of disconnect from the divine, being out of touch with your soul, you may find yourself struggling with ego in the material world. That's because the universal life force is blocked. You're not letting life in. Your life then becomes rigid and fixed in beliefs, eventually manifesting in your body as stagnation, from impaired energy and blood flow to the buildup of chemical or emotional toxins.

The health of your skin becomes an indicator of these happenings. Acne may begin to surface, along with acute bouts of eczema. Eczema has actually been coined "skin asthma" in Eastern teachings, because of its correlation with the lungs and conditions of dampness. Skin conditions tied to the crown energies include acne, eczema, psoriasis, rosacea, and dry skin.

As we begin to explore eating to nurture the crown chakra energies and restore energy flow, the first step is detoxification. Remember— everything begins from somewhere on the inside. The process of healing requires going from the inside out.

Food for the Crown Chakra

Nourishing the crown chakra energies involves detoxification, fasting, and balancing hormones.

Detoxification is the process by which the body gets rid of toxins to create the best inner environment for regeneration and renewal. The body, a self-healing entity, continually seeks newness. This metabolic process brings you to your purest form, which is the essence of the crown chakra.

Detoxification is orchestrated by the liver with the assistance of secondary organs such as the skin, lungs, and kidneys in a complex process to regenerate and purify your inner workings. If you have ever given up coffee, you have felt the body's detoxification process in headaches, fatigue, and moodiness. The process of renewal and releasing buildup in the body, whether chemical or emotional in nature, involves a period of time when you experience some discomfort. The body is eliminating excess, meaning you go out of balance in order to find a new space of health.

Many clients that I work with want to feel better, but the thought of dealing with the detoxifying process makes them resistant to undergoing a program. The common belief is they should not feel discomfort because they were changing their diet to healthy foods, so therefore they should automatically feel good.

Detoxification takes effort and self-discipline, not the most marketable qualities, so the concept of doing a cleanse has been presented in the food industry as a more convenient detox option. But cleanses are not passive actions; they can place a lot of demand on your body's reserves and systems. If your bodily functions are already compromised and overworked, you must ask if this is appropriate for you. A cleanse can add more stress than help for the body.

Detoxification is about shifting eating habits and lifestyle choices, not trying to find a quick fix to jump-start your health. The reality is, your body detoxifies on its own without your assistance. The choices you make regarding your eating and lifestyle habits either support or hinder the process.

Most people get wrapped up in weight on the scale and think a cleanse or fast is the answer to seeing those numbers go down. Will you drop some quick weight by doing a cleanse? Yes, however the weight loss will be transitory. It's not fat weight, rather water and a little protein from your muscles, guaranteed to lower your metabolic rate and make long-term weight loss success less attainable.

Fasting takes on different intentions and methods, depending on if it's a part of a mainstream cleanse, the thought processes of TCM or Ayurveda, or a cultural tradition like the Muslim holiday of Ramadan. Fasting does not have to require the extreme of not eating at all. Sometimes fasting means shifting to a diet of cruciferous vegetables for a few days or only eating up to a certain hour each day. Remember everyone has a different constitution, which means some approaches to eating are more appropriate and others less tolerable, depending on your makeup. This is why bringing awareness to your relationship with food is so important. You need to find what works for you.

What does detoxification look like when choosing and eating food? It is a consistent diet that supports immunity, gets blood and energy moving, and heals the digestive tract. The first step is to remove toxins from your food supply. Eat fresh foods, organic whenever possible, while removing all processed and refined foods from your diet. Eat nothing that comes in a package or box. Put down the bakery goods and on-the-go meals. It's time to eat light and bright, straight from nature and ideally plant-based. I will go ahead and wave the vegan flag for this level of consciousness.

Plants are blessed with phytonutrients, those health-supportive compounds that will assist in the regeneration and renewal processes of all your cells. They also have that alkaline-forming quality that assists in keeping the body in an oxygenated state, supporting the self-healing process. Recall animal-based foods are the slowest in vibration, grounding, and providing connection to Earth. Here at the crown chakra, it's the highest vibration, a liberating energy that is connecting you to the divine. Think plants, sunlight, and oxygen.

The detoxification process is also the first step to balancing your hormones. As you begin shifting your overall inner state of being, hormones shift as well. They are part of the holistic network, communicating with the whole through infinite connection. You can begin this process by removing toxins from your food supply as mentioned above and through the restoration of your digestive system.

Digestion is most efficient and effective when foods are warm and cooked, so consider stepping away from a dietary pattern that is filled with chilled, cold, or raw foods for a while. The digestive tract is a living environment, making prebiotic foods to feed your friendly microbiome, an essential part of detoxification and immunity. Add some unpasteurized sauerkraut or fermented veggies to your diet. Some raw garlic or red onion will do the trick too.

All Flavors. All flavors play a role in the crown chakra energies. When looking to balance the body's inner workings, bringing it to its purest form, every aspect plays a part. In keeping with the holistic paradigm, everything is connected and plays a part in a larger dynamic.

Keep the bitter flavor front stage with an abundance of leafy greens to assist in detoxification and overcome stagnancy. A little sour flavor through the use of lemons or limes will stimulate the digestive juices and aid in digestion. The pungent flavor of onions and garlic are great for stimulating circulation and the health of the lungs, skin, and liver. Keep the sweet flavor in the form of grains, such as millet, legumes, and cooked vegetables. A small amount of salt, not from the salt shaker but from the addition of seaweed, has a cooling and moistening effect to combat dryness. Again, keep the diet diverse, light, and bright.

Purple and White Colors. All colors resonate with the crown chakra. Many see the crown chakra as the vibration of purple, but it is also viewed as white, signifying the accumulation of all colors. The crown blends all the chakra's energies, forming the highest vibration. Eat a rainbow diet with the more deep and dark colors the better.

Strategies for Balance

A food strategy for the crown chakra is to detoxify and cleanse the physical body, bringing you to your purest possible form. In that state, you see past your physical body to where your soul connects to the Universe.

I recommend that in the weeks surrounding a season change you stop eating after five o'clock in the evening. This gives your body an opportunity to recycle and detox what is already in it while preparing your body for nature's next cycle. Depending on how you respond to that experience, you may wish to explore this intermittent fasting once or twice each week for the remainder of the year. Do a little experimenting.

When I suggest this intermittent fast, many clients immediately ask if it is dangerous. The reaction reveals how attached we may be to the concept of structured eating, a conditioned belief that food is required every three hours for a person to be healthy. That's actually a current marketing myth to boost your metabolism, a common weight-loss strategy. It's an interesting theory, but one without scientific backing.

What happens when you eat in so structured a manner is your body becomes less adaptable and flexible. *You* become less adaptable and flexible! Of course, you will feel different than the norm when you go without a meal, but that's the point—creating a difference. Can you sit in that discomfort? Can you sit in the change, so you can feel more than your physical body? I promise you will not go malnourished or starve from not eating after five in the evening for a period of a few weeks around the season's change. You will also feel lighter. You may even look forward to your next nighttime fast in the future.

I mentioned earlier about using your kitchen as your next meditation studio. Grab a recipe, or better yet be creative with ingredients in the fridge and just start cooking. It doesn't need to be a complex meal or use any advanced technique. It doesn't matter if you are boiling water for quinoa—just do it fully with your undivided attention and awareness of that very task. You will receive benefits of relaxation, lowering of anxious states, heightened awareness, and pure enjoyment.

Gratitude Exercise

How you perceive the world changes everything about your life. You actively choose your thoughts, beliefs, and perceptions. What if every day you wrote down fifteen things that you are grateful for? Not your new pair of sneakers that you scored a sale on. Go deeper.

At first you may be stumped, thinking, *How can I possibly find fifteen things to be grateful for?* It can at first seem like a high number. But give it a whirl. You'll be surprised once you get going how the list takes off and becomes truly endless.

To go one step further, add five things that you are grateful for that have not yet happened. Through the crown chakra, you are connected directly to the Universe. Let your imagination run and feel it! The most important action is to *feel* it. The Universe will do everything possible to manifest in your physical world your thoughts fueled by sincere gratitude.

Crown Chakra Strategies for Balance

- Consume a plant-based dietary pattern, no animal products.
- Choose foods from nature, nothing processed.
- Incorporate cruciferous vegetables into daily meal choices.
- Put all flavors in your dietary pattern.
- Eat a rainbow diet, unifying the chakras.
- Drink plenty of filtered water; some with freshly squeezed lemon.
- Add prebiotic food, such as raw, unpasteurized sauerkraut, to your dietary pattern.
- Have your largest meal of the day at lunch.
- Consider late-day fasting in weeks surrounding a season change.
- Have gratitude for your meals.

Self-Reflective Questions

Arriving at the crown chakra, your relationship with food is about expanding your perception within the holistic paradigm. This means grasping that food not only has physical properties, energetic characteristics, and environmental factors but also impacts every cell of your being. Food takes on a meditative quality, a space of gratitude, and an invitation to meet your most authentic self. Be open to possibilities and to removing your fixed beliefs on food and life in general. Let the universal consciousness in. Take the time to reflect on the questions below.

1. Are you experiencing any physical illnesses reflective of the crown chakra?
    a. Are you experiencing headaches or migraines?
    b. Do you find your toxic load is high and in need of a cleanse?
    c. Do you struggle with a neurological disorder?
    d. Are you finding your coordination and balance declining?
    e. Is getting a good night's sleep a challenge for you?
    f. Do you have or have you had a brain tumor?
    g. Have you been told you have pituitary/hypothalamus gland dysfunction?
    h. Are you challenged with learning disabilities?
    i. Do you have any skin issues?
2. Are you open to new ideas about food and life?
3. Do you think you know best and find yourself quashing others' beliefs?
4. Do you sit in gratitude for your meals?
5. Do you live in the present moment or a past/future story?
6. Have you ever considered fasting to feel yourself past your physical needs?
7. Have you had the pleasure of meeting your soul?
8. Do you truly operate from a holistic paradigm? First with food, then with life?
9. Are you a person of faith, having a trust in the Universe's bigger plan?
10. Do you consider yourself a spiritual being?

Stage 3 Self-Assessment Tool

Here is the complete self-assessment tool to help you unravel the hidden messages in food and begin finding connections in your life—to food, the external world, and your most authentic self.

Use the questions below as a scan to do daily, preferably in the morning as you are getting ready for your day.

1. Overall, how are you feeling (present, relaxed, calm, distracted, anxious, annoyed, or other)?
2. How are your energy levels (ready to go, light and alert, tired, heaviness in body, or other)?
3. Are you feeling internally hot or cold? How do your hands and feet feel?
4. Are you hydrated?
5. How are your bowel movements (diarrhea, constipated, daily frequency, or other)?
6. Do you feel dry (skin, throat, digestive system), or do you feel damp (bloated, swelling, congested)?
7. Was your diet in the past day more alkaline or acidic?
8. Have your recent meal choices been more whole foods or more processed?
9. Are you eating a lot of animal? Any particular one?
10. What environment are you eating your meals in (peaceful, disruptive, with company, alone, or other)?
11. What season is it? What element is dominant? How about physical organs?
12. What is the weather outside like (hot, cold, rainy, dry, or other)?
13. What is your internal weather (overheated, cold, congested, dry, or other)?
14. How are you incorporating the flavor of the season into your meals?
15. What cooking techniques would be the most serving of your health goals today?
16. Do you feel centered and grounded today?
17. Are you resisting any change in your life right now?

18. What food has control of your will today? Where does your craving lie?
19. What is one commitment surrounding your relationship with food you will practice today?
20. What are you grateful for today?

AFTERWORD

Looking Forward

Congratulations! You have successfully completed your journey through the three stages of transforming your relationship with food. Within each stage, the hidden messages in food are revealed to you, giving you the opportunity to expand your perspective on food to include your body, mind, and soul.

Within the physical food on your plate is a map that reveals messages for you on all levels of who you are. Remember food is a reflection of who you are and how you are living. Your daily food choices, cravings, aversions, and eating environments and behaviors all have messages for you. Just think with each connection you make in your life's map, you will be revealing another dimension of who you are. With each step you take toward understanding yourself, you are bringing the healing process into action.

Food is the initiator of your healing process. By embracing the full power of food with all its traits, physical and energetic in nature, you are nourished holistically. This is the key to living this holistic journey, knowing you are a body, mind, and soul. You are designed to create and grow on all levels of being—physical health, cognitive skills, emotional integrity, and the evolution of your soul. Your relationship with food is the pathway to take you there!

If this understanding remains at the forefront of your mind, all of your life choices—whether in food, health, or life circumstances—will be made authentically, which is the underlying gift of this journey.

Your body will thank you for the increased variety of nutrients available, making the renewal of every single cell in your body an easier and healthier process. Your energy, blood, and physiological systems respond with glee to diversity. Your beliefs surrounding food begin to expand. Your mind becomes open to possibilities. This creates a space for you to begin stepping outside your comfort zones. Your soul is all smiles when you transform your relationship with food. You are letting life in. It is a pathway to overcome fears, have new experiences, and connect with your authentic, whole self.

Embracing the full potential of food, eating in sync with the seasons, and aligning your food choices with your Higher Self is a journey, one that never ends. To this day, I rely on each of these three stages of the journey to guide me, whether in making an immediate food choice, planning ahead for the current season, or reflecting on a deeper life lesson that sits before me.

Keep in mind that as you expand your perspective on food, your entire life expands to meet and include your new perspective. As you continue to use this book as a guide, you will create the space to heal and connect more deeply with your true nature.

I am excited for you to begin. You certainly deserve to receive all the benefits of discovering the hidden messages in food. I offer my sincerest wishes as you set out on the amazing journey to live your authentic life. I look forward to the time when our paths cross.

Namaste.

HEALTH-SUPPORTIVE SOUP RECIPES

Food is an incredible initiator of the healing process with the kitchen a training space to practice living more expansively. Allow your kitchen experience to be a space to add diversity, creativity, and peace into your life.

Remember—recipes are guidelines, not strict rules. Here I share with you my favorite soup creations. I encourage you to deviate from the recipes. Change up the ingredients as much as you wish. If you are a garlic lover, throw in a few more cloves! Have extra veggies in the fridge? Add them to a recipe. Feel the freedom and playfulness that creating meals can bring.

Barley Lentil Soup

Yields: 6 cups

1 tablespoon coconut oil
1 cup (4 ounces) leeks, white and light green parts, chopped
1 cup (4 ounces) onion, chopped
1 cup (4 ounces) celery, chopped
1 cup (4 ounces) carrots, chopped
1 cup (3 ounces) fennel bulb, stems removed, bulb chopped
1 tablespoon garlic (about 3 cloves), minced
1 teaspoon fennel seeds, ground
1 teaspoon dried thyme
5 cups vegetable stock
3/4 cup green lentils, rinsed
1/2 cup barley, hulled
2 tablespoons fresh lemon juice
1/4 cup fresh parsley, chopped
pinch of red pepper flakes (optional)
sea salt and freshly ground pepper to taste

1. In large pot, heat coconut oil over medium heat. Add the leeks, onions, and a pinch of sea salt, sauté until they begin to soften, about 3 minutes. Add celery, carrots, and fennel and continue to sauté, stirring frequently until the carrots begin to soften, about 6–8 minutes. Add garlic, fennel seed, and thyme and cook for another minute.

2. Add stock, lentils, and barley and bring to a boil. Cover, lower to a simmer, cook until lentils and barley are soft, about 40–50 minutes.

3. Add lemon juice, parley, and red pepper flakes. Stir, cook for another minute. Season with salt and pepper to taste.

Beet Apple Soup

Yields: 6 cups

1 tablespoon coconut oil
1 cup (4 ounces) onion, chopped
2 cups (3/4 pound) beets, peeled and chopped
2 cups (1/2 pound) carrots, peeled and chopped
2 tablespoons garlic cloves (about 4), minced
2 fuji apples (about 3 cups), peeled and chopped
4 cups vegetable stock
3/4 cup coconut milk
2 tablespoons fresh lemon juice
1/4 cup fresh parsley, chopped
sea salt and freshly ground pepper to taste

1. Heat coconut oil in pot over medium heat, adding onions with a pinch of sea salt. Cook, stirring frequently, until onions begin to soften, about 3 minutes.

2. Add the beets and carrots, cooking until carrots begin to soften, stirring frequently, about 8 minutes. Add garlic, cook for another minute.

3. Add apples, stock, and coconut milk and bring to a boil. Cover and lower to a simmer, for about 45 minutes, or until beets soften.

4. Blend soup. Using a handheld blender is the easiest choice, or you can also transfer to food processer to blend and return to pot.

5. Add lemon juice and parsley, cooking for another minute. Seasoning with sea salt and freshly ground black pepper to taste.

Broccoli Avocado Soup with Pumpkin Seed Pesto

Yields: 6 cups

1 tablespoon coconut oil
1 cup (4 ounces) onion, diced
1/2 cup (2 ounces) celery, chopped
1 tablespoon garlic (about 3 cloves), minced
1/4 teaspoon cayenne
6 cups (1 pound) broccoli, chopped
5 cups vegetable stock
1 avocado (about 1 cup), mashed
1 tablespoon tamari
1/4 cup cilantro, minced
1–2 tablespoons lemon juice
sea salt and freshly ground pepper

Pesto
1/2 cup pumpkin seeds
1/4 cup olive oil
1 cup (2 ounces) basil, minced
1/2 cup (1 ounce) parsley, minced
1 teaspoon garlic (about 1 clove), minced
2 tablespoons lemon juice
sea salt and freshly ground pepper

1. In large pot, heat coconut oil over medium heat. Add the onions, celery, and a pinch of sea salt, sauté until begin to soften, about 3–5 minutes. Add garlic and cayenne, cooking another minute. Add broccoli, stirring frequently until broccoli begins to turn bright green, about 1–2 minutes.

2. Add stock and avocado. Cover and bring to a boil. Lower heat and simmer for 20 minutes, or until broccoli softens.

3. Meanwhile, place all pesto ingredients into food processor. Blend and put aside.

4. Add tamari, cilantro, and lemon juice to soup. Using a handheld blender, blend the soup (or transfer to food processer to purée and return to pot).

5. Season with sea salt, freshly ground black pepper, and more lemon juice to taste. Drizzle pesto on soup when serving.

Black Bean and Sweet Potato Soup

Yields: 6 cups

1 tablespoon coconut oil
1 cup red onion, diced
1 tablespoon garlic, minced
1 tablespoon jalapeño, minced
1/2 cup celery, chopped
1/2 cup carrot, chopped
1 teaspoon cumin seed, ground
1 teaspoon oregano, dried
1/4 teaspoon cayenne pepper
1/4 teaspoon paprika
4 cups black beans, cooked
1 cup sweet potato, peeled, diced
1 cup tomatoes, chopped
4 cups vegetable broth
2 cups spinach, coarsely chopped
1/4 cup parsley, minced
2 tablespoons lemon juice
sea salt
freshly ground black pepper

1. Heat coconut oil in a large pot over medium heat. Sauté onion with a pinch of sea salt until translucent, about 3 minutes.

2. Add garlic, jalapeño, celery, carrots, and spices, and cook until carrots begin to get tender, about 6–8 minutes.

3. Add beans, sweet potato, tomatoes, and broth to the pot. Bring to a boil and then lower heat to a simmer and cook for about 15 minutes, or until sweet potato begins to get tender.

4. Add spinach, parsley, and lemon juice. Cook until spinach begins to wilt, about 1–2 minutes.

5. Add sea salt, black pepper, and additional lemon juice to taste.

Corn Chowder with Chickpeas

Yields: 6 cups

1 tablespoon coconut oil
1 cup (4 ounces) onion, diced
1/2 cup (2 ounces) carrot, chopped
1/2 cup (2 ounces) red bell pepper, chopped
2 cups (1 pound) red potato, cut into 1/2-inch cubes
1 tablespoon garlic (about 3 cloves), minced
1 teaspoon cumin
1/2 teaspoon turmeric
3/4 teaspoon paprika
3 cups vegetable stock
1 cup coconut milk
3 cups (12 ounces) fresh or frozen corn
1 1/2 cups chickpeas, cooked
1/4 cup (1/2 ounce) fresh parsley, minced
1 to 2 teaspoons lemon juice, to taste
pinch of red pepper flakes (optional)
sea salt and freshly ground pepper to taste

1. In large pot, heat coconut oil over medium heat. Add the onions and sauté until they begin to soften, about 3 minutes. Add carrots, bell pepper, and potatoes and continue to sauté, stirring frequently until the carrots begin to soften, about 8 minutes. Add garlic, cumin, turmeric, and paprika and cook for another minute.

2. Add stock, coconut milk, and corn. Bring to a boil, cover, and reduce to a simmer for 20 minutes.

3. Using a handheld blender, puree 1/2–3/4 of the soup (or transfer to food processer to purée and return to pot).

4. Add chickpeas and parsley. Season with lemon juice, red pepper flakes, sea salt, and freshly ground pepper.

Curry Sweet Potato and Kabocha Squash Soup

Yield: 8 cups

1 tablespoon coconut oil
1 1/2 cups (8 ounces) onion, diced
2 tablespoons garlic, minced
2 tablespoons ginger, minced
4 cups (1 pound) sweet potatoes, peeled, diced
4 cups (8 ounces) kabocha squash, peeled, diced
1 tablespoon cumin seed, ground
1 teaspoon coriander seed, ground
1/2 teaspoon turmeric
1/4 teaspoon cinnamon, ground
1/4 teaspoon cardamom, ground
1/4 teaspoon cayenne
6 cups vegetable stock
1 cup coconut milk
1 tablespoon maple syrup
1 tablespoon lemon juice
sea salt and freshly ground pepper to taste
bunch of baby arugula (optional)

1. In large pot, heat coconut oil over medium heat. Add onions and a pinch of sea salt and sauté until translucent, about 3 minutes. Add garlic and ginger, sautéing for another minute. Add sweet potato and squash, continuing to sauté until they begin to soften, about 8–10 minutes. Add spices, coating vegetables and cooking for another minute.

2. Add stock and bring to a boil. Cover, lower to a simmer, and cook until sweet potatoes and squash start to fall apart, about 20 minutes.

3. Using an immersion blender, puree the soup (or transfer to food processer to purée and return to pot). Add coconut milk and maple syrup. Continue to simmer another two minutes. Add lemon juice. Add sea salt and freshly ground pepper to taste.

4. Serve hot with handful of arugula on top (optional).

Garden Vegetable Soup

Yields: 15 cups (I love to make this one in bulk and freeze half)

1 tablespoon olive oil
2 cups (8 ounces) onion, diced
1 cup (4 ounces) celery, chopped
1 cup (4 ounces) carrot, unpeeled, chopped
1 cup (9 ounces) red potatoes, medium diced
1 tablespoon garlic (about 3 cloves), minced
1 cup (4 ounces) orange bell pepper, diced
1 tablespoon oregano, dried
1 teaspoon basil, dried
1 teaspoon paprika
8 cups vegetable stock
4 cups kidney beans, cooked
2 cups (8 ounces) tomatoes, deseeded, chopped
2 cups (8 ounces) zucchini, medium diced
1 cup (4 ounces) green beans, trimmed, chopped into 1-inch pieces
1 cup peas, fresh or frozen
2 cups (7 ounces) broccoli, chopped into bite-size florets
1 cup brussels sprouts (4–5 sprouts) cut in half, then cut into thin strips
(or separate leaves whole)
2–3 tablespoons fresh lemon juice
1 teaspoon red pepper flakes
1/4 cup fresh parsley, minced
sea salt and freshly ground black pepper

1. In a large pot, heat oil over medium heat. Sauté onion with a pinch of sea salt until translucent, about 3 minutes. Add celery, carrot, potatoes, garlic, and bell pepper. Continue to sauté until carrots begins to soften yet keep their texture, about 5–8 minutes.

2. Add oregano, basil, and paprika, toss to coat vegetables, and cook for another minute.

3. Add stock, beans, tomato, zucchini, and green beans. Simmer uncovered for 15 minutes to combine flavors.

4. Add peas, broccoli, and brussels sprout leaves, cooking until broccoli turns bright green and slightly tender (do not let broccoli get soft), about 3 minutes.

5. Stir in 2 tablespoons lemon juice, red pepper flakes, and parsley. Season with sea salt and freshly ground black pepper. Adjust with additional lemon juice and seasonings.

Leek Potato Soup with Broccoli

Yields: 8 cups

1 tablespoon coconut oil
4 cups (3–4) leeks (white and light green parts), thoroughly washed, roughly chopped
1 1/2 pounds (2 heads) broccoli, peel stalks, cut stalks/stems and florets into bite-size pieces, separate stalks/stems from florets
1 pound red potatoes, unpeeled, diced
1 tablespoon garlic, minced
6 cups of vegetable broth
1 bay leaf
1 cup of coconut milk
2 tablespoons lemon juice
1/2 teaspoon cardamom
sea salt and freshly ground black pepper

1. In large pot, heat coconut oil over medium heat. Add the leeks and sauté until begin to soften, about 3 minutes. Add broccoli stalks/stems and continue to sauté, stirring frequently until broccoli stems begin to soften, about 8 minutes. Add potatoes and continue to sauté until they begin to soften, about another 4–5 minutes. Add garlic and cook for another minute.

2. Add broth and bay leaf. Bring to a boil, cover, and reduce to a simmer for about 20 minutes, until potatoes and broccoli stems completely soften. The potatoes will start to fall apart.

3. Using a handheld blender, purée the soup (or transfer to a food processor to blend and return to pot). Add coconut milk and broccoli florets into soup and continue simmer until florets turn bright green and slightly tender, about 2 minutes. Make sure not to overcook the broccoli florets.

4. Add lemon juice and cardamom. Simmer another 2 minutes. Season with sea salt and freshly ground pepper.

Miso Soup

Yields: 4 cups

kombu, 1 sheet, cut into 2-inch pieces
1/2 cup chard, roughly chopped into bite-size pieces
2 ounces shitake mushrooms, stemmed, sliced
1 tablespoon fresh ginger, grated
1/4 cup miso paste
1/2 cup (1 ounce) scallions, chopped
1/2 teaspoon red pepper flakes (optional)
a splash of tamari soy sauce (optional)

1. Over medium heat, add kombu to pot with 4 cups of water. Heat until the water is about to boil. The kombu will start to open up and float to surface.

2. Lower to a simmer and add chard, mushrooms, and ginger to the broth and simmer for 5 minutes.

3. Meanwhile make a slurry with the miso. Take some liquid from the pot and using a small bowl, slowly mix the miso paste in. Add the slurry to the pot. Turn off heat. Add scallions.

4. Optional is adding a sprinkle of red pepper flakes and a splash of tamari before serving.

Moroccan Spiced Lentil Soup

Yields: 8 cups

1 tablespoon coconut oil
1 cup onion, diced
1 cup orange bell pepper, diced
1 tablespoon fresh ginger, peeled and grated
1 tablespoon garlic, minced
1 teaspoon cumin seed, ground
1/2 teaspoon coriander seed, ground
1/2 teaspoon allspice, ground
1/4 teaspoon turmeric
1/8 teaspoon cloves, ground
1/4 teaspoon cayenne
2 cups black beluga lentils, rinsed
6 cups vegetable stock
1 cup coconut milk
2 cups (3 ounces) spinach, chopped
2 teaspoons fresh lemon juice
1/4 cup parsley or cilantro, chopped
sea salt
freshly ground black pepper

1. In a medium skillet, heat coconut oil on medium-high heat, sauté onion with a pinch of salt until translucent, about 3 minutes. Add bell pepper, ginger, and garlic, sautéing for another 4 minutes, until bell pepper begins to soften. Add spices, toss to coat vegetables, and cook for a minute.

2. Add lentils and broth; bring to a boil. Lower to a simmer, cook, slightly covered, for 20–25 minutes, or until lentils become al dente.

3. Add coconut milk and spinach, allowing spinach to wilt, about 1–2 minutes.

4. Add lemon juice, parsley, salt, and pepper. Adjust seasoning to taste.

Mung Bean Soup

Yields: 6 cups

1 cup dry mung beans, soaked overnight
1 tablespoon olive oil
1 1/2 cups (6 ounces) onion, diced
1 cup (4 ounces) celery, chopped
1 cup (4 ounces) carrot, chopped
1 tablespoon (about 3 cloves) garlic, minced
1 tablespoon fresh ginger, minced
1 teaspoon cumin seed, ground
1 teaspoon coriander seed, ground
1 teaspoon turmeric
5 cups vegetable stock
1 cup tomatoes, seeded, chopped
1 cup (6 ounces) sweet potato, peeled, cubed
1/4 cup cilantro, minced
2 tablespoons lemon juice
sea salt

1. Place mung beans in a medium-size bowl, cover with water, and soak overnight.

2. In a large pot, heat oil over medium heat. Sauté onion with a pinch of sea salt until translucent; about 3 minutes. Add celery, carrot, garlic, and ginger, and continue to sauté until carrots begin to soften yet keep their texture, about 5–7 minutes. Add cumin, coriander, and turmeric, tossing to coat vegetables with spices, and cook for an additional minute.

3. Add stock, tomatoes, and previously prepared mung beans. Bring to a boil. Lower heat and simmer uncovered. After 20 minutes, when mung beans are almost tender, add the sweet potato, simmering until sweet potato softens, another 5 minutes or so.

4. Add cilantro and lemon juice and simmer for another minute. Season with sea salt to taste.

Navy Bean Soup

Yields: 6 cups

1 tablespoon coconut oil
1 cup (4 ounces) leeks, white and light green parts, chopped
1/2 cup (2 ounces) celery, chopped
1/2 cup (2 ounces) carrots, chopped
1/2 cup (2 ounces) orange bell pepper, chopped
1 tablespoon garlic (about 3 cloves), minced
8 ounces fire-roasted diced tomatoes, drained
1 teaspoon oregano, dried
3 leaves sage
2 teaspoons fresh thyme
1 quart vegetable broth
4 cups navy beans, cooked
1 tablespoon tamari
1 bunch (6 ounces) escarole (or spinach, arugula, watercress, chard)
squeeze of fresh lemon juice
sea salt and freshly ground black pepper

1. In a large pot over medium heat, sauté leeks in coconut oil with a pinch of sea salt until translucent, about 3 minutes. Add celery, carrots, and bell pepper, cooking until carrots begin to soften, about 8 minutes. Add garlic, sautéing for another minute. Add tomatoes and herbs, stir well, and cook for a few more minutes to incorporate flavors.

2. Add the broth and navy beans. Season with sea salt, freshly ground black pepper, and tamari. Simmer for 15 minutes.

3. Add greens to the soup, simmering until they turn bright green, about a minute. Season with salt and pepper. If it tastes flat, add a squeeze of lemon juice. Remove sage before serving.

Ratatouille Soup

Yields: 10 cups

1 tablespoon olive oil
1 cup (4 ounces) onion, diced
1/2 cup (2 ounces) celery, chopped
1 tablespoon garlic (about 3 cloves), minced
1 small jalapeño (about 1–2 tablespoons), deseeded, minced
1 cup (7 ounces) orange bell pepper, diced
1 cup (5 ounces) yellow summer squash, medium diced
1 cup (6 ounces) eggplant, peeled, medium diced
2 cups (8 ounces) zucchini, medium diced
1 teaspoon oregano, dried
1 teaspoon basil, dried
6 cups vegetable stock
2 cups tomatoes, deseeded, chopped
4 cups cannellini beans, cooked
1/4 cup basil, minced
1/2 teaspoon red pepper flakes
2 tablespoons lemon juice
sea salt and freshly ground black pepper

1. Heat oil in a large pot over medium heat. Sauté onion with a pinch of sea salt until translucent, about 3 minutes. Add celery, garlic, jalapeño, and bell pepper and continue to sauté until celery begins to soften yet keeps its texture, about 5 minutes.

2. Add summer squash, eggplant, and zucchini, cooking for another 5 minutes, stirring frequently. Add oregano and basil, toss to coat vegetables, and cook for another minute.

3. Add stock, tomatoes, and beans. Bring to a boil. Lower heat and simmer uncovered for 20 minutes to combine flavors.

4. Add basil, red pepper flakes, and lemon juice and simmer for another minute. Season with sea salt and freshly ground black pepper to taste.

Soba Bok Choy Soup

Yields: 6 cups

1 tablespoon coconut oil
1 cup (8 ounces) leeks, white and light green parts, chopped
1/2 cup (2 ounces) carrots, chopped
1/2 cup (2 ounces) celery, chopped
1 tablespoon garlic (about 3 cloves), minced
1 tablespoon fresh ginger, grated
6 ounces baby bok choy, stems and leaves separated and chopped
4 cups vegetable broth
3/4 ounce lemongrass, sliced and crushed
1 kaffir leaf
1 cup organic edamame, shelled
2 ounces soba noodles
2 tablespoon mirin
1 tablespoon tamari
1/2 cup (1 ounce) scallions, chopped
sea salt and freshly ground black pepper to taste

1. In large pot, heat coconut oil over medium heat. Add the leeks and sauté until they begin to soften, about 3 minutes. Add carrots and celery and continue to sauté, stirring frequently until the carrots begin to soften, about 8 minutes. Add garlic, ginger, and bok choy stems, stirring for another 1–2 minutes.

2. Add stock, lemongrass, kaffir leaf, and edamame and bring to a boil. Cover and simmer for 15 minutes.

3. Add soba noodles, cooking for 3 minutes. Add mirin and tamari and cook another 2 minutes or until noodles are just about done.

Be careful not to overcook. Noodles should be cooked through but not mushy.

4. Add bok choy leaves and scallions, heating until leaves turn bright green, about 1 minute.

5. Season with sea salt and freshly ground black pepper to taste.

White Bean, Cabbage, and Kale Stew

Yields: 6 cups

1 tablespoon coconut oil
1 cup (6 ounces) onion, diced
1 cup (2 ounces) loosely packed leeks, chopped
1 cup (3 ounces) carrots, medium diced
1 cup (3 ounces) parsnip, medium diced
1 cup (3 ounces) celery stalks, medium diced
1 tablespoon garlic (about 3 cloves), minced
3 juniper berries, crushed
1 teaspoon thyme, dried
1/2 teaspoon allspice, ground
1 teaspoon caraway seeds
1 teaspoon cumin, ground
4 cups cooked great northern beans (or navy beans)
1 cup fresh tomatoes, chopped
4 cups (1 pound) cabbage, shredded
1 cup (8 ounces) sweet potato, peeled, medium diced
2 bay leaves
6 cups vegetable stock
3 cups kale, coarsely chopped, bite-size pieces
2 tablespoons apple cider vinegar or lemon juice
sea salt and freshly ground pepper to taste

1. Heat oil in large pot over medium-high heat. Sauté onions and leeks with a pinch of sea salt until translucent, about 3 minutes.

2. Add carrots, parsnip, celery, and garlic, and sauté until carrots begin to soften, about 8 minutes. Add the juniper, thyme, allspice, caraway seeds, and cumin, and cook for 1 minute, stirring frequently.

3. Add beans, tomatoes, cabbage, sweet potato, bay leaves, and stock, and bring to a boil. Cover and simmer for 30 minutes or until vegetables are tender.

4. Add kale and continue to cook until it starts to wilt and turn bright green, about 2–3 minutes.

5. Add acid of choice, 1 teaspoon at a time. Adjust with additional acid, salt, and pepper to taste.

RECOMMENDED READING

Aggarwal, Bharat. *Healing Spices*. New York: Sterling Publishing, 2011.

Chodron, Pema. *Living Beautifully: With Uncertainty and Change*. Massachusetts: Shambhala, 2013.

Chopra, Deepak. *Ageless Body, Timeless Mind*. New York: Harmony, 1994.

Colbin, Annmarie. *Food and Healing*. New York: Random House Publishing, 1986.

Dispenza, Joe. *Evolve Your Brain*. Florida: Health Communications, Inc., 2007.

Dispenza, Joe. *You Are the Placebo*. California: Hay House, 2015.

Dooley, Mike. *Leveraging the Universe*. New York: Atria Books / Beyond Words, 2012.

Flaws, Bob. *The Tao of Healthy Eating*. Colorado: Blue Poppy Enterprises, 2013.

Lipton, Bruce. *The Biology of Belief*. California: Hay House, 2005.

Myss, Caroline. *The Anatomy of Spirit*. New York: Three Rivers Press, 1996.

Myss, Caroline, and Norman Shealy. *The Creation of Health*. New York: Harmony, 1998.

Ni, Maoshing. *The Yellow Emperor's Classic of Medicine*. Massachusetts: Shambhala, 1995.

Pert, Candace. *Molecules of Emotion*. New York: Simon and Schuster, 1999.

Pert, Candace. *Your Body Is Your Subconscious Mind*. Colorado: Sounds True, 2005.

Pitchford, Paul. *Healing with Whole Foods*. California: North Atlantic Books, 2002.

Schinn, Florence. *The Wisdom of Florence Scovel Shinn*. New York: Simon and Schuster, 1989.

Sternberg, Esther. *The Balance Within*. New York: W. H. Freeman and Company, 2001.

Tolle, Eckhart. *The New Earth: Awakening to Your Life's Purpose*. New York: Penguin Books, 2008.

Williams, Roger. *Biochemical Individuality*. New Jersey: John Wiley & Sons, 1998.

Wrangham, Richard. *Catching Fire: How Cooking Made Us Human*. New York: Basic Books, 2010.

Zukav, Gary. *The Seat of the Soul*. New York: Simon and Schuster, 1990.

ACKNOWLEDGMENTS

In gratitude to my editor, Nancy Marriott, for helping put my thoughts and vision on paper. Thank you for not only your editing expertise but your patience and enthusiasm about this project. To everyone at Balboa Press, I thank you for your talents and commitment to this creation. Every helping hand I needed along the way arrived, without hesitation, and in kindness.

I sit in gratitude to those in my life who have shared their support, acted as a sounding board for my ideas, helped me remain grounded through the process, laughed with me, and ultimately created a space where I knew this was possible. I honor all of you.

Jeri, I thank you for your unwavering support, friendship, editing assistance, and love for the bobby pin. Lance, every thoughtful and supportive action you have made has touched my heart. Kate, you always understand my thinking process and that grounding has been such a resource for me. Mandy, our parallel lives have been a source of love, playfulness, support, and growth. I am eternally grateful. CT and Jane, your friendship continues to be one of acceptance and support that helps me feel that anything is possible. Maribeth and Margaret, thank you for all the support, laughter, and adventures that have helped me throughout these years. Joanie, thank you for always keeping it real. Your honesty and laughter has carried me through so much change. Eileen, I cherish our friendship and all the support and laughter we can exchange. Grace, what a gift you have been in my life all these years. Thank you for being you. Bec and Cher, my favorite yogis, your practices and genuine hearts grounded me as I was challenged through this creation. I also thank Micki, Mom, Joey, Kim, Katie, Craig, Lindsay, Mico, the Loturcos, and Stimpfels. All of you played a part in making this book possible. Again, I honor and thank you.

INDEX

ABOUT THE AUTHOR

Teri Mosey, PhD, is an international speaker, consultant, and health-supportive chef who has been working in various arenas of the health and wellness industry since 1996. Her background includes biochemistry laboratory research, exercise prescription design for therapeutic programs, holistic nutrition consulting and education, culinary demonstrations and hands-on cooking events, and speaking engagements for allied health professionals and community members around the world.

Teri's knowledge and expertise has developed over the years to include the ancient teachings of traditional Chinese medicine, India's chakra system to our most current understandings of mind-body physiology and quantum physics. Her career began with a bachelor's in biochemistry and a master's in exercise physiology. Over the years, Teri's perspective expanded, opening doors to Eastern teachings and leading to the completion of a PhD degree in holistic nutrition, along with certification from the Chef's Training Program at the Natural Gourmet Institute in New York, the top health-supportive culinary school in the United States.

Teri has presented keynotes, breakout sessions, and weeklong retreat events for organizations that include IDEA Health & Fitness Association, Fitness Innovations Thailand, Canadian Fitness Pro events, Academy of Applied Personal Training Education, JCC Manhattan, Hofstra University, Golden Door Spa, and Apple Inc. In addition to speaking engagements, Teri offers holistic living coaching experiences and online courses with built-in guidance.

Teri's mission is to assist others in discovering their personal paths to wellness. She passionately believes that anyone equipped with a dynamic foundation of knowledge, combined with personal responsibility and freedom of choice, can recognize the power within to cocreate their health and ultimately their life.

Connect with Teri at https://www.terimosey.com.

CPSIA information can be obtained
at www.ICGtesting.com
Printed in the USA
LVHW01s1600160918
590318LV00002B/265/P